AYR
COAST

THE OFFICIAL GUIDE BOOK

JAMES A BEGG

Published by the Rotary Club of Ayr

What tho, like commoners of air,
We wander out, we know not where,
But either house or hal'?   but = without
Yet Nature's charms, the hills and woods,
The sweeping vales, and foaming floods,
Are free alike to all.

Robert Burns

www.ayrshirecoastalpath.org

AYRSHIRE COASTAL PATH SPONSORS

South Ayrshire Waste
and Environment Trust

SCOTTISH
NATURAL
HERITAGE

NORTH AYRSHIRE
COUNCIL

JOIN THE MOVEMENT

irvinebay

the National Trust
for Scotland

a place for everyone

Dedication:
For my wife Helen who has endured much,
but will one day walk and love 'that bloody Path.'

All Proceeds from sales of this book
are donated by the Author to the Rotary Club of Ayr
for local and overseas Rotary charity work.

Published by the Rotary Club of Ayr

ISBN 978-0-9559063-0-5

First Published in 2008 by Rotary Club of Ayr, Scotland

Printed By Kestrel Press, Irvine, Scotland

The maps used in this publication are reproduced by permission of Ordnance Survey on behalf of the Controller of Her Majesty's Stationery Office, ©Crown Copyright 2008. All rights reserved.
Ordnance Survey Licence Number100048147.

Digital mapping from Dotted Eyes ©Crown Copyright 2008.
All rights reserved. Licence Number 100019918.

PUBLICATION

The Rotary Club of Ayr would like to acknowledge the very substantial financial contributions towards the cost of publication of this book by -

Scottish Enterprise Ayrshire
17 Hill Street, Kilmarnock
Tel: 01563 526623
www.scottish-enterprise.com

Alex Begg & Co., Ayr
Cashmere Mill Shop
17 Viewfield Road, Ayr
Tel: 01292 267615
www.beggscotland.com

Craig Tara Holiday Park
Dunure Road, Ayr
Tel: 01292 265141
www.craigtaraholidaypark.com

Due to their combined generosity, the proportion of the Proceeds of the Guide Book available for donation to charity is now considerably more than it would otherwise have been - for which we are most grateful.

Photographs: Our grateful thanks to Mike Blair for his beautiful iconic cover photograph of an 'Arran Twilight' taken from Doonfoot; to Alastair Swan for his equally evocative 'Arran Sunset with Tree' taken from the Carrick Hills; and to Colin Mearns, The Herald, for his 'Men at Work' - proof that Rotarians can actually get their hands dirty! Unless otherwise acknowledged, the rest of the photographs were taken by Rotarians Jimmy Begg, Willie Watters, and Bernard Cotton.

THE AYRSHIRE COASTAL PATH ROUTE

Total Length = 161 km = 100 miles from GLENAPP to AYR to SKELMORLIE (including essential detours to Burns Heritage Park, Dundonald Castle Visitor Centre and Kilwinning Abbey).

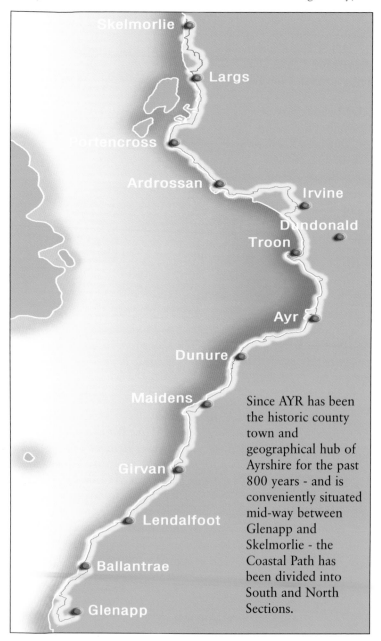

Skelmorlie

Largs

Portencross

Ardrossan

Irvine

Dundonald

Troon

Ayr

Dunure

Maidens

Girvan

Lendalfoot

Ballantrae

Glenapp

Since AYR has been the historic county town and geographical hub of Ayrshire for the past 800 years - and is conveniently situated mid-way between Glenapp and Skelmorlie - the Coastal Path has been divided into South and North Sections.

CONTENTS

PAGE

7. Introduction

10. Pointers to the Path

15. Responsible Access

16. Advice to Walkers – Be Country-wise

18. GLENAPP - BALLANTRAE
Distance = 13.5 km = 8.3 miles *Moderate/Difficult*

26. BALLANTRAE – LENDALFOOT
Distance = 10.5 km = 6.5 miles *Moderate/Difficult*

34. LENDALFOOT - GIRVAN
Distance = 10.5 km = 6.5 miles *Moderate/Difficult*

42. GIRVAN - TURNBERRY - MAIDENS
Distance = 13.0 km = 8.1 miles *Moderate/Easy*

54. MAIDENS - CULZEAN CASTLE - DUNURE
Distance = 10.0 km = 6.2 miles *Moderate/Easy*

64. DUNURE - THE ANCIENT ROYAL BURGH OF AYR
Distance = 14.3 km = 8.9 miles *Moderate/Difficult*

81. Branch Detour to ROBERT BURNS BIRTHPLACE
MUSEUM (Local Path)
Distance = 3.8 km = 2.4 miles *Easy*

84. AYR Tourist Office - PRESTWICK - TROON
Distance = 12.5 km = 7.8 miles *Easy*

94. TROON - Short Beach Route -
ANCIENT ROYAL BURGH OF IRVINE
Distance = 10 km = 6 miles *Easy*

104. TROON - Inland Detour - DUNDONALD CASTLE
(Local path)
Distance = 7.6 km = 4.1 miles *Easy*

104. DUNDONALD CASTLE – ANCIENT ROYAL
BURGH OF IRVINE
Distance = 11.5 km = 7.1 miles *Easy*

CONTENTS

110. IRVINE - KILWINNING - STEVENSTON -
SALTCOATS - ARDROSSAN
Distance = 17.5 km = 10.8 miles   *Easy*

122. ARDROSSAN - SEAMILL - PORTENCROSS
Distance = 10.5 km = 6.5 miles   *Easy*

128. PORTENCROSS - FAIRLIE - LARGS
Distance = 11.5 km = 7.1 miles   *Easy*

136. LARGS -
a) 'High Road' - SKELMORLIE
Distance = 15.0 km = 9.3 miles   *Moderate*

144. b) 'Low Road' - SKELMORLIE
Distance = 11.5 km = 7.1 miles   *Easy*

146. Acknowledgements

148. Bibliography

149. Appendix I   -   Tidal Information

152. Appendix II -   Checklist of Ayrshire Coastal Path Birds

156. Appendix III -   Planned Stranraer to Glenapp route
Planned Wemyss Bay to Glasgow route

CHANGES OF ROUTE IN THE FUTURE:

The long-term success of the Ayrshire Coastal Path depends on trust, goodwill and co-operation between walkers and landowners. All route descriptions contained in this Guide Book the time of going to print are based on this co-operation, and fixed at this point in time. However, it is always possible that a change of landowner, change of mind, or change of circumstance could lead to a local change of path route at a future date.

If no alternative route is offered, walkers should still be able to exercise their legal right of responsible access to cross any land gap, using the most sensible and appropriate alternative route.

The Official Website of the Ayrshire Coastal Path will be updated regularly, and if in doubt, walkers are advised to consult it for information on any possible Path changes. **www.ayrshirecoastalpath.org**

INTRODUCTION

During the recent magical BBC series 'Coast', which brought home to a broad public the outstanding beauty and diversity of our British coastline, viewers had an interesting opportunity to sample on the small screen, many of our existing long-distance coastal walks – from Northumbria to Cornwall and Pembrokeshire. While undeniably beautiful, diverse and spectacular, they all had something in common which detracted a little from their appeal – an unbroken, uninteresting, flat sea horizon.

In contrast, the eyes of travellers walking northwards along the Ayrshire Coastal Path from Glen App to Skelmorlie, with sun and wind in their backs, will gaze constantly on one of the finest panoramic coastlines in the British Isles. Rising remote and sheer from the exposed grey open waters of the Lower Firth of Clyde, Ailsa Craig - that mysterious granite volcanic plug known to thousands of passengers to Ireland as Paddy's Milestone - dominates the mid-firth, while beyond it to the west the horizon is straddled by the hazy blue outlines of the Kintyre peninsula and Sanda, and to the southwest, the cloud-capped faint low smudge of the Antrim coast of Northern Ireland.

The perspective slowly but constantly changes as 'The Craig' draws abreast at Girvan then falls astern, and the distant jumbled mountains of Arran gradually assume the iconic reclining profile of the 'The Sleeping Warrior' - as Auld Ayr and Irvine give way to Ardrossan and walkers close to within eight miles of the Isle of Arran. To the north of Ardrossan, Arran in turn falls slowly astern as Fairlie and Largs draw near, its rugged mountains gradually obscured by the Isles of Cumbrae, while looming Largs Hills now conspire with the Isle of Bute and the high hills of the Cowal Peninsula to embrace the yacht-speckled, sheltered waters of the Upper Firth.

Though vague ideas about an Ayrshire Coastal Path had apparently been around for years, the concept was never actively pursued till December 2003, when, I was asked by the Rotary Club of Ayr (www.rotary-ribi.org) as their Centenary Project Convenor to come up with a suitable project **to celebrate the Centenary of Rotary International** - founded in Chicago in 1905 by Paul Harris, an American lawyer, as a community-based and worldwide Service Organisation.

[Rotary International is now the world's largest service organisation with a membership of over 1.2 million men and women Rotarians in 168 countries. Apart from its well-known local and overseas charity work, Rotary pioneered Polio Plus, and for the past twenty years in partnership with WHO and Unicef, has been at the forefront of this worldwide campaign to eradicate the scourge of Polio from the world.] (www.rotary.org)

Our original modest plan was for a simple walkers' path from Ayr to Dunure, but the notion quickly developed to extend it south along Croy beach to Culzean Castle. Then with a sudden serious rush of blood to the head, came the realisation that it was virtually all beach walking from there to Girvan – and likewise northwards from Ayr to Largs! This left only the small matter of finding suitable routes from Girvan to Glenapp in the south, and from Largs to Skelmorlie in the north - and the rest . . . as they say . . . is history – and a lot of hard work!

First Steps - Jimmy Begg and John Davidson surveying Dipple Shore

The first two years were spent surveying possible routes and visiting and obtaining the consent of all the farmers and landowners along the proposed path. The ultimate success or failure of the project depended entirely on their goodwill – and their willingness to take the risk of allowing a long-distance path over their land.

It was our mutual good fortune that the Land Reform (Scotland) Act 2003 became law around this time, which greatly clarified the position of both walkers and landowners with regard to their rights and responsibilities. The crux of the Act is that *walkers shall be responsible at all times for their own actions and safety of themselves and others while walking the countryside,* and this is the basis on which the Ayrshire Coastal Path has been established. We cannot thank enough all those farmers and landowners who so kindly and generously gave their consent for this major project.

After lobbying and consulting South and North Ayrshire Councils and the new Countryside Access Forum, the concept of an Ayrshire Coastal Path was finally adopted as part of South Ayrshire Council's Access Strategy in 2005 - the Rotary International Centenary Year. But unfortunately, as with so many other projects, although we had strong 'support in principle' from both Councils when we presented our survey findings, major council funding proved impossible.

Undeterred - and having discovered that we could source funding ourselves - in April 2006 we grasped the nettle and decided to undertake the entire project on our own, reckoning that because we already had 65 miles of tracks and proms, and 30 miles of beach, only around 5 miles of new field-edge path needed to be established, most of which would be simple beaten-earth path. Since voluntary labour was also to be used for much of the path clearance work, *the set-up costs would be relatively modest.*

A management group – the Ayr Rotary Coastal Path Group (ARCPG) – was constituted to enable us to apply for funding, in which we were very successful, raising £66,000 from South Ayrshire Waste Environmental Trust, Scottish Natural Heritage, South Ayrshire Council Rural Fund, North Ayrshire Council Landfill Tax Fund and Community Outdoor Access Grant Scheme.

Although most of the route infrastructure was already in place, work parties (mainly retired Rotarians) had to clear two 200 - 400-metre sections of thorny jungle and build two new beach access paths down steep escarpments between Heads of Ayr and Dunure; survey and contract for the erection of 61 kissing gates, two small bridges, two causeway fords, and short sections of fencing; the installation of 47 waymarker posts and hundreds of waymarker signs – many of them shared with Sustrans along urban sections where the Path links with the NCN7 and NCN73.

An Official Website www.ayrshirecoastalpath.org had to be set up, brochures and Information Boards designed and the Guide Book written and published.

From the confirmation of our first tranche of grants in October 2006, the completion of the 100 miles of Coastal Path has taken only eighteen months, and cost around £70,000. A huge amount of work was involved, but at the end of the day, it has all been worthwhile.

Ayrshire now has a wonderful, scenic and historic Coastal Path which will provide her ain folk with *health-giving recreational exercise and an educational opportunity to experience and cherish their own countryside*, while at the same time adding another important dimension to the Ayrshire tourist portfolio and attracting a great number of walking visitors as guests in our bonny county.

This Guide Book is not just a step-by-step route-marker; it is a celebration of the history, the geography, social development and natural history of the Ayrshire Coast. Its compilation was a voyage of discovery for the Author, which hopefully will provide a stimulus for all those who read it to venture outdoors on their own personal journey.

As the young wife of one of our Ayrshire farmers pertinently and generously observed - *'We are only the stewards of the land we work, for those who follow on.'* With eyes open and senses alert to the natural beauty around them, I hope that these words and this book will inspire all walkers with a similar desire to protect and cherish the increasingly fragile world in which we live, and which one day our children will inherit.

Jimmy Begg. Project Coordinator

Topography:

If measured like a bowstring across the sea from Glenapp to Skelmorlie, the latitudinal length of the County of Ayrshire is 55 miles, while its concave curved coastline measures 84 miles (134 km). Including essential detours to Robert Burns Birthplace Museum, Dundonald Castle Visitor Centre, and Kilwinning Abbey, the overall length of the Ayrshire Coastal Path will total 100 miles.

Apart from the rugged hill country to the south and north, the topography of the broad bights of Ayr and Irvine Bays, with their low-lying hinterland, provides an almost uninterrupted beach walk from Girvan to Largs, which covers three-quarters of the coastline. All the major rivers, Stinchar, Girvan, Doon, Ayr and Irvine – and the Pow Burn - have been bridged near their mouths.

In the remote hilly south, long stretches of cliff from Glen App to Ballantrae; from Bennane Head towards Lendalfoot; at Kennedy's Pass north of Lendalfoot; and sections from Culzean Castle to Dunure and Heads of Ayr, where the Carrick Hills descend to the sea; are the only places where walking along the shore itself is difficult or impossible. In the first areas there are good estate tracks and remnants of old pack roads, which effectively bypass the cliffs and provide superb high-level views of the Firth; while nearer Ayr are sections of the old Ayr-Turnberry railway line which provide a conduit through parts of this agricultural area. In the central, low-lying and populous section to the north of Ayr, most of the walk will be on natural shore terrain, and along paths and promenades in urban areas where there is already a right of public access. North of Largs, the route once more takes to the hills for the final scenic stretch to Skelmorlie.

Over small but fairly crucial sections between Glenapp, Girvan and Ayr – and north of Largs - corridor paths needed to be established through sensitive farmland and several golf courses to provide access links between beaches, and the entire success of the project is largely due to the generous consent of those farmers, landowners, and golf clubs. At Culzean, South Ayrshire Council and the National Trust for Scotland have allowed the route to run through the Country Park from Maidens to Croy beach.

Heritage Sites:

1) *Historical:* Coastal Ayrshire has a tremendous range of historical sites, from the fantastic – such as 'Sawney Bean's Cave' at Bennane Head and Tam o Shanter's Auld Brig o Doon; to the factual - the historic coastal castles of Ardstinchar, Turnberry, Culzean, Dunure, Greenan, Dundonald, Seagate, Ardrossan, Portencross and Kelburn. In the course of their journey along the coast, walkers will encounter evidence of human activity from the Stone Age to the Nuclear Age. Bronze age settlements, Roman camps, Iron Age duns, Norman mottes - and medieval castles attacked by Vikings, visited by Mary Queen of Scots, demolished by Cromwell, or rebuilt by Robert Adam - all give testimony to our turbulent past and whet the imagination.

For its size, over the centuries Ayrshire has punched well above its weight with its great contribution to both Scottish - and world - history and development. As well as being our Rotary International Centenary Year, 2005 was also the 700th Anniversary of the death of Sir William

Wallace, and the year 2006 celebrated the 700th anniversary of the crowning at Scone near Perth of Robert the Bruce as King of Scotland. Both these famous heroes of Scottish history were born in Ayrshire, and are intimately connected with many historic sites along the Path.

The year 2005 also celebrated the 800th Anniversary of the granting of the Royal Charter to the town of Ayr by William III of Scotland. Since Ayr has always been the county town and hub of Ayrshire, we felt this also merited recognition. In Ayr, St John's Tower, Cromwell's Fort, Loudoun Hall, Lady Cathcart's House, the Auld Kirk and the Auld Brig, are all within a few yards of the Tourist Office in Sandgate.

Scotland's most famous son, her National Bard, Robert Burns, was born in the village of Alloway - and the Path makes a short essential detour from Greenan Castle Bay to visit Burns' Cottage and the Robert Burns Birthplace Museum. (www.burnsheritagepark.com).

The birthplace of the Stuart Dynasty of Scottish and British Kings and Queens is to be found at Dundonald Castle near Troon – another important detour.

Irvine has the Scottish Maritime Museum and Seagate Castle; Kilwinning, has its Abbey; and Largs celebrates its Viking connections with the Vikingar Centre.

2) *Industrial:* Small boulder-cleared sandy bays where the earliest fishing boats were hauled ashore; snug wee fishing harbours; large 18-19th Century industrial ports; and finally the huge deep-water terminal at Hunterston, all bear witness to the evolving stages of Ayrshire's long maritime history. The coastline still bears evidence of the fishing, saltpans, coalmining, iron works, shipbuilding, and explosives industries of the past, and the pulp mills, distilleries, aerospace, chemical and IT industries of the present.

3) *Sporting:* Primarily - Golf, Golf, Golf. Blessed with many miles of sand dunes ideal for traditional links courses, Ayrshire has been called the Home of Golf ever since the *first-ever* Open Championship was played here at Prestwick. Although the sport is often described by non-gowfers as 'a good walk spoiled', walkers on the Coastal Path will be fascinated and honoured that the route crosses or skirts three of the most famous Open Championship links courses in the world – Turnberry, Prestwick, and Royal Troon.

However, for Curling enthusiasts, Ailsa Craig merits special mention as the source of the granite for all the world's curling stones, which are made in Mauchline, Ayrshire.

Natural History:

Because of its compact size, and the amazing diversity of terrain and habitat experienced when travelling even short distances, Scotland plays host to a far greater number of bird species than would be found if travelling over the same distance in the USA, Australia, or continental Europe.

The diversity of terrain encountered while traversing the Ayrshire Coastal Path mirrors that of Scotland itself, and the sea and seashore, the cliffs, the hills and moors, the rivers and estuaries, woodlands and open pastures all have their favoured bird species. The checklist at the end of the Guide Book lists 135 species, but this is by no means a final tally for keen birdwatchers. *(See Appendix II).*

Similarly, for the amateur botanist there is a wide variety of flowers, trees and shrubs to be encountered in these diverse habitats; and geology enthusiasts will also enjoy the fine range of sedimentary, conglomerate and igneous rock formations, and raised beaches, exposed by glaciation and incessant pounding of the seas over millenia.

Wild goats, roe deer, seals, porpoises, otters, foxes, white hares, stoats and weasels, will often be seen by quiet and observant walkers. *To see wildlife, avoid wearing bright garish colours, keep quiet and alert, and walk in small groups of 2-6 people.*

Transport:

Car: The entire length of the walk is well served by roads running parallel to the coast, providing excellent access by private car. All day-walking sections have some parking facilities at either end for two-car parties.

Bus: Services are frequent and regular to all towns and villages en route, *and walkers are encouraged to reduce their carbon footprints (and expense) by using public transport.* The Path Website has links to Stagecoach bus timetables. (www.stagecoachbus.com)

Train: Services from Glasgow to Ayr and Stranraer cover all coastal towns from Kilwinning to Girvan, with a branch service north from Kilwinning to Largs. The service from Glasgow to Wemyss Bay covers the northern section of the walk. The Path Website links with Scotrail timetables. (www.firstgroup.com/scotrail)

Plane: Glasgow Prestwick Airport is only a few hundred yards from the Path, with excellent train and bus links for visitors flying in to Prestwick from England or abroad. (www.gpia.co.uk)

Boat: PO Ferries run from Stranraer or Troon to Ireland, (www.poscottishferries.com), and Calmac from Ardrossan to Arran, Largs to Cumbrae, and from Wemyss Bay to Bute. (www.calmac.co.uk) All these ports are on the route, and Ardrossan and Wemyss Bay can provide linkages with established walks on Arran and Bute. Once again, there is a Path Website link with PO Ferries and Caledonian McBrayne.

Amenities:

Since villages or towns are seldom more than five to eight miles apart - all with shops, restaurants, or pubs - there is no shortage of provision and eating facilities – and public toilets. In addition, there are numerous caravan and camping sites at regular intervals to cater for back packers, and plenty of B&B, guesthouse and hotel facilities. The Website has an Accommodation link. (www.visitscotland.com)

The Walking:

Easy Walking - From Ayr northwards to Largs, most of the walk is easy and suitable for all age groups - along natural beach terrain, cycle paths and pleasant coastal town promenades.

Moderate Walking - From to Glen App northwards to Ayr, although much of the coast is also fine beach walking, there are many sections of coast - the cliffs north of Glen App; Bennane Head north of Ballantrae; at Kennedy's Pass north of Lendalfoot; from Croy Bay to Heads of Ayr, where the Carrick Hills descend to the sea - where walking along the shore itself is difficult or impossible. Luckily in some areas there are gradual ascents over estate tracks and remnants of ancient pack roads, and also level sections of disused railway line, that effectively bypass the cliffs and provide superb high-level views of the Firth.

Difficult Walking - Unavoidably - between Ballantrae and Girvan, Girvan and Turnberry, Culzean and Dunure, and Dunure and Ayr - there are several short (150-300 m) sections of route that involve scrambling over a rocky shoreline. While passable at most states of the tides, these can be impassable in some places for up to 1-2 hours before and after certain high spring tides (but only on 3-5 days each month). Detailed advice is given in each <u>Section Guide</u> of the <u>Guide Book</u> and delays can be eliminated by careful route planning, taking this advice into account, and by checking the Admiralty Easy Tide Tables (http://easytide.ukho.gov.uk). *(See Appendix I)*

Time Allowance – Although it is easy to cover ground at 3-4 miles per hour, please give yourself plenty of time to stop and eat, watch wildlife, take photographs and enjoy your surroundings - by allowing about 1 hour for every 2 miles. E.g. 4-5 hours for 8-10 miles.

Path Users:

Due to our low-cost strategy of simply linking existing sandy beaches and rough passable shore terrain by utilising existing field-edge paths, wrack roads, farm tracks, pack roads and old railway track - *the Ayrshire Coastal Path is essentially a practical 'route' rather than a laid-out formal path. Consequently, and especially in the south, it is primarily a path geared only for well-equipped agile walkers, since many stretches along cliff-tops, up gullies and over rough stony beaches are not suitable for cyclists, horses, or slip-on shoes!*

However, being mainly on the level and with few steep hill climbs, compared with other established long distance walks, the Ayrshire Coastal Path is designed to be enjoyable – not challenging. This less challenging aspect, and its easily accessible 6-8 mile (10-15 km) short stages, should make it attractive to *properly-equipped* locals and tourists - young family groups, school groups, and middle-aged and veteran day-walkers - as well as the more energetic long-distance backpackers who may choose to walk two or more sections in a day.

In some areas, walkers may wish to linger for several days, exploring the surrounding countryside and sampling other walks such as the River Ayr and Carrick Ways. Some may wish a sail to Ailsa Craig from Girvan, a trip on the Waverley from Ayr, a ferry trip across to Arran from Ardrossan, or to Millport from Largs; or enjoy sightseeing visits to tourist attractions such as the proposed Ailsa Craig Centre at Girvan, Culzean Castle, tthe Robert Burns Birthplace Museum in Ayr, the Dundonald Castle Centre, the Maritime Museum at Irvine, and the Vikingar at Largs.

From Ayr to Largs most of the route can be cycled since the National Cycle Network routes NCN7 and NCN73 run parallel with or form a good part of the Coastal Path.

Many of the adjacent sandy beaches in the middle and north sections are already used for horse riding.

For wheelchair users, many paths within Culzean Country Park, all beach promenades, most of the NCN cycleways from Ayr to Ardrossan - and the roadside pavement between Ardrossan and Seamill - are smooth enough for wheelchairs.

Walking Connections

a) *Local Linking Paths:*

While not part of the official Path, the Guide Book describes several optional detours, which are highly recommended – to the Robert Burns National Heritage Park (www.burnsheritagepark.com), Dundonald Castle (birthplace of the Stuart Dynasty) (www.dundonaldcastle.org.uk), and Kilwinning Abbey. There are also several local farm hill paths geared for the more energetic walker, that provide wonderful panoramas of the Firth of Clyde. The Round Cumbrae Walk can be done in a day via the Largs - Cumbrae Ferry.

b) *Long-distance Ways:*

1. The Ayrshire Coastal Path complements and links up with the River Ayr Way recently completed from Glenbuck to Ayr (www.theriverayrway.org) - and also with the Carrick Way at present being planned and constructed in the Girvan hinterland. (www.carrickway.co.uk)

2. In the south, the Rotary Club of Stranraer is actively engaged at present in developing a 10-mile footpath from Stranraer to Glenapp to link the Ayrshire Coastal Path with the Southern Upland Way. (www.southernuplandway.com)

3. Summer day trips from Girvan provide an opportunity to land on and climb Ailsa Craig.

4. A local walking route from Wemyss Bay via the Kelly Cut to Cornalees Park Centre in Clyde Muirshiel Regional Park was established and signposted in autumn 2007, effectively extending the range of the Ayrshire Coastal Path round the Greenock Cut to above Greenock. (www.clydemuirshiel.co.uk)

5. From here it could easily be extended eastwards to the Erskine Bridge and along the Forth and Clyde Canal to Maryhill – with the whole forming a **Clyde Coastal Path** in which the Ayrshire Coastal path would link up the Southern Upland Way and the West Highland Way. (www.west-highland-way.co.uk). *[At time of publication, Inverclyde Rotary Clubs are actively considering our approach to see if they would be willing to pioneer this section – to complete a Rotary-organised Path from Stranraer to Glasgow].*

6. The Arran Coastal Way (www.coastalway.co.uk) can be accessed via the Ardrossan - Brodick ferry service.

7. The West Island Way round Bute (www.visitbute.com) is accessed via the Wemyss Bay – Rothesay Ferry.

The Guide Book Maps are small scale and should be used in conjunction with the following detailed maps.

The following Ordance Survey Maps are advisable:
Landranger 1 : 50,000 sheets 76, 70, 63
Explorer 1 : 25,000 sheets 317, 326, (333), 341

RESPONSIBLE ACCESS

All walkers using the Ayrshire Coastal Path do so at their own risk and are expected to take responsibility for their own actions, the safety of themselves and their companions, the welfare of livestock and wildlife, and the avoidance of damage to crops in the land through which they must pass – as laid down in the recommendations of the Scottish Outdoor Access Code which followed on the Scottish Land Reform Act of 2003.

While the Ayr Rotary Coastal Path Group has taken every care to ensure that the path route it has established is as safe as possible under the constraints imposed by a few landowners, our function has been simply to facilitate the setting up of this long-distance path. Our agreements with all landowners have been of an informal nature, based mainly on the mutual benefits to both proprietors and walkers of having an easily defined route across working farms and estates, which minimises risk of disturbance to livestock and crops, and risks to the safety of walkers.

All walkers should have read the SOAC leaflet:- 'Know the Code before you go.'
www.outdooraccess-scotland.com

The Ayr Rotary Coastal Path Group cannot accept responsibility for any accident or injury sustained by walkers using the Ayrshire Coastal Path.

Descending to Currarie Port, Glenapp Estate

Dwellings: Please respect people's privacy and peace of mind. When passing close to houses or farm dwellings please do so quietly and quickly and with a minimum of fuss.

Gates: Field gates should be left as you find them, whether open or closed. Kissing gates have been built next to almost every field gate on the Path, minimising the need for walkers to open or close field gates anywhere on the route.

Dogs: Dogs especially, can cause cattle to act in protective and aggressive manner, and they should be kept on a very short lead and where possible be led through an adjacent field away from large animals. If animals become aggressive, let dog off lead and make your own way calmly to safety. Preferably, in areas with livestock, dogs should be left at home.

Livestock: Care should be taken before crossing through any field of livestock to check if there may be a bull with the cows. Cows with young calves are just as dangerous as bulls, and walkers (*especially with dogs*) should never get between a cow and its calf. The hill areas north of Largs, between Ayr and Culzean, and from Girvan to Glenapp are most sensitive to disturbance. It is recommended that dogs be left at home.

Lambing: On the coast, lambing takes place between January and the beginning of May, and it is recommended that walkers should avoid fields where lambing is taking place, and keep their dogs controlled on a close lead at all times. The hill areas north of Largs, between Ayr and Culzean, and from Glenapp to Girvan are most sensitive to disturbance. It is recommended that dogs be left at home.

Large Groups: Large numbers of noisy, brightly clad walkers disturb both the livestock and the wildlife, *and it is debatable whether a group of 30-40 people really conforms to the concept of 'Responsible Access'.* Crocodiles are scary! While the ideal number is probably 3-4 people, this is not always practicable. However, in the South Section, *we recommend that walk leaders should break up large parties into groups of six or less*, and start them off at 5-minute intervals – or get half their group to walk in from either end of the section - if they really want to enjoy seeing any wildlife on their walk. North of Ayr, there is really no great problem till above Largs, when the same advice would apply.

Kit: Walkers must be properly shod and prepared for the terrain over which they travel, and should have planned their trip beforehand. Trainers or slip-on shoes may be suitable for the sandy shores and promenades of the north, but walking boots are essential south of Ayr. If negotiating slippery shore rocks, a walking pole is advisable for balance.

Weather: While the Ayrshire coastline may be beautiful in sunshine, it can be very exposed in foul weather, and wind and waterproof clothes should be carried if there is any prospect of rain. For an up-to-date Met Office forecast please click on to (www.metoffice.gov.uk/weather)

Tides: At several points on the South Section– which are highlighted on both Maps and Brochures - trips should be timed carefully to avoid being trapped for 1-4 hours by rising tides on several days around the period of High Spring Tides, (which occur every two weeks at the times of the New and Full Moons). **Simple and careful planning will avoid stupid and unnecessary delays. Packing a pair of plimsolls would allow easy wading.** Refer to Appendix I, which gives clear guidance on understanding Ayrshire coast tides - in conjunction with the Admiralty EasyTide Website - http://easytide.ukho.gov.uk. Great care must be taken to check <u>the tide tables for Ayr.</u>

N.B. *Daytime Spring Tides are much higher in late Autumn and Winter than during Summer months.* The Website also has a link with Admiralty EasyTides.

Breeding Shorebirds: From May to July, it is extremely important on narrow compressed coastal strips *that walkers make every attempt to walk on the sand <u>below the tide-line</u> where possible - and try to avoid tramping on shingle patches above high water mark.* This precaution is to minimise the high risk of crushing the nests of oystercatchers and ringed plovers, whose camouflaged motionless chicks, or clutches of speckled eggs on gravel, are almost invisible. Always be on the lookout for breeding birds running silently down the beach from HWM away from their nests. If they are calling around you, you are too close! So watch your feet and look out!

Litter: In three hours on a blustery Saturday morning in March 2007, the Rotary Clubs of Ayr, Alloway, Prestwick, Troon and Girvan combined with over a hundred willing volunteers, to clear the walking beaches from Girvan to Troon of over 900 bags of rubbish accumulated over many years. Without this superb effort, future walkers on the Path might have found that the distraction of crunching through drifts of plastic bags and drinks bottles - comprising 75% of the total litter - would have completely destroyed their enjoyment of the magnificent scenery around them.

To make sure that this won't happen, each spring all the coastal Rotary Clubs from Girvan to Largs now organise an annual Great Rotary Beach Clean, enthusiastically assisted by members of the public and youth groups. Walkers on the Path will find this wee verse on most of the kissing gates along the route to encourage them to help us to protect the environment.

> *The Ayrshire Coastal Path*
>
> *Be ye Man - or Bairn - or Wumman,*
> *Be ye gaun - or be ye comin,*
> *For Scotland's Pride - no Scotland's shame,*
> *Gether yer litter - an tak it Hame!*

Read it – and do it!

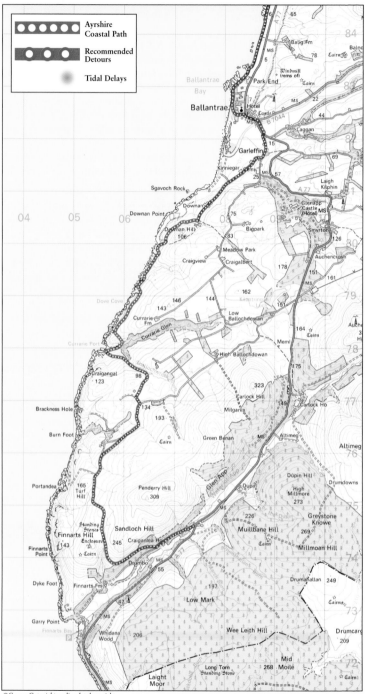

Ayrshire
Coastal Path

Recommended
Detours

Tidal Delays

18

GLENAPP - BALLANTRAE

1. Glenapp Kirk – Sandloch Hill track - Glendrisaig - Craigans - Currarie Port - Downan Hill – Old Stinchar Brig – BALLANTRAE Harbour

Distance = 13.5 km = 8.3 miles   Time: 4 - 41/2 hours

Car Parks: **Glenapp car park is small. Suggest parking cars at Foreland, Ballantrae, then take bus to Glenapp and walk back.**

Walking Summary: *Moderate/Difficult* - 200m and 150m ascents over rough estate roads, grassy cliff-top, livestock, farm tracks and minor roads.

Points of Interest:	
Transport:	Good hourly bus service
Historical:	Prehistoric cairns, enclosure and standing stones Smuggling coves Ardstinchar Castle
General:	Contrasting wild upland and superb cliff walk seascapes
Nature:	Coastal birdlife and diverse flora Remnants of ancient woodland Salmon of River Stinchar
Eating provisions:	Ballantrae Cafe and Inn
Public Toilets:	Ballantrae - Foreland
Accommodation:	B&Bs and Hotel at Ballantrae (Check www.ayrshirecoastalpath.org)

Afore ye gang: Throughout the 14th to 18th Centuries, any traveller heading north from Castle Kennedy would have faced the long journey up through wild Carrick with fear and foreboding. This was Kennedy country, a lawless land, ruled by the powerful Kennedys for hundreds of years with a ruthlessness born of being above the law of the King. Indeed, the Earl of Cassilis *was* the Law, and the self-styled King of Carrick. Peel towers and castles every few miles bore witness to Kennedy power and control, and many had a 'dule tree' nearby on which any miscreants who offended their feudal rulers would be hanged.

Before the Reformation, the route south through Ayrshire to Galloway - and the return trip - was also one of royal pilgrimage by James IV and later Mary Queen of Scots, heading for the Priory at Whithorn where St Ninian established the first Celtic Christian church in Scotland around 400 AD; and there are a number of castles and houses along the Path in which those royal pilgrims lodged during their outward and return journeys. For twenty-first century travellers, the danger of death still lurks round every corner of that long winding road - in the shape of thundering traffic on the A77 (T) heading to and from the ferry terminal at Stranraer. Apart from a few occasions when the Path has, of necessity, to cross or run parallel to this busy road, walkers should be free to relax and enjoy the magnificent coastal views and pastoral peace of the Ayrshire countryside, and steep their imaginations in the momentous history of this southwest corner of Scotland - famously known as 'The Cradle of Scots Independence' - but not to forget that:

> *'Twixt Wigtoune and the town of Aire,*
> *And laigh down by the Cruves of Cree,*
> *You shall not get a lodging there*
> *Except ye court a Kennedy.*   *laigh=low*

Well, not quite! There is ample and good accommodation, and a warm and friendly welcome, everywhere along the Ayrshire Coastal Path.

Tangible evidence of the ancient Kennedy heritage is present in the many ruined coastal castles, each with its tale to tell of family vendettas, blood feuds, turf wars, hostage-taking, murder, torture, intrigue and treachery. And in this present troubled world, it would seem that our modern 21st century has not progressed very far from the medieval mores of the fifteenth!

Glenapp Kirk

20

Walking: However, the walkers' introduction to Ayrshire is a peaceful but energetic one, leading as it does through the beautiful land and seascapes of Glenapp estate. Travelling north on the A77, the tiny Glenapp Kirk - reputed one of the smallest in Scotland - lies on the right side of the road three kilometres north of the Ayrshire county boundary. Opposite, on the left side of the road is the turn off to a roadside cottage - and a small car park beyond, formed from a stretch of disused roadway.

This is the starting point for the Ayrshire Coastal Path which runs left down to the Bridge of the Mark over the Water of App. In May and early June the hillside above provides a spectacular display of purple and pink rhododendrons. About 0.5 km further along, the farm track forks right and leads uphill through woodland to emerge around the 200 metre contour at a sheepfold between Blarbuie and Sandloch Hills on the edge of heather covered grouse moor, which in August is a quilt of purple, and where occasionally there may be a rare glimpse of hunting merlin or hen harriers. In January, colour is still provided by gorse in bloom. To the left, on Blarbuie is a prehistoric cairn, enclosure, and standing stones. From here onwards are wonderful views of Loch Ryan busy with fast ferries; Corsewall Lighthouse at the north end of the Rhinns of Galloway; and the distant low blue outlines of Ireland and the Mull of Kintyre. The upland track provides good level walking conditions over sheep and hill cattle grazings for the next 3 kms, passing through several kissing gates, bypassing Glendrisaig Farm which lies half-hidden down the hillside to the left, and curving round the end of a finger of woodland which extends north east from the steading.

Heading uphill from Glenapp

Walkers are advised not to take dogs over this section from Glenapp to Ballantrae. Lambing takes place from February till early May, and in the past ewes have been startled and separated from their lambs at a vulnerable stage. During the summer, hill cattle on the grazings do not take kindly to the presence of dogs, especially if they have calves, and could possibly attack both dogs and their owners.

Just beyond the copse, turn left off the road down a smaller track, which quickly takes a sharp right bend to run past the poignant ruin of an old cottage, then follows the Shallochwreck Burn down to Currarie Port.

The grassy margins of the bay provide an ideal place for a picnic stop and an opportunity to drink in the peace and tranquillity of this delightful spot. On a calm spring morning, the low moan of eider drakes is broken only by the rush of wavelets breaking on the flat shingle, the anxious piping of nesting oyster-catchers, and the deep croak of a raven passing overhead. Patches of tiny white stonecrops and clumps of sea pink decorate the rocks. It is very likely that a flock of wild goats will be grazing on the slopes - the billies have impressive horns, but a retiring nature. The height of the shingle bank and tossed timbers testify to a very different winter scenario and the power of north-westerly gales. Yet on a crisp clear mid-winter day, Currarie Port does provides shelter from easterly winds for a comfortable lunch stop. In the eighteenth century, these small out-of-the-way 'ports' strung along the Ayrshire coast would be frequently used by brandy, tea, and tobacco smugglers.

Glenapp cliff walk with Bennane Head in distance

Follow the new estate track that conveniently crosses a pipe bridge over the burn and traverses up the promontory called on the 1:25000 map by the strange name of Donald Bowie (not David!). The steep sides of Currarie Glen guard a fine remnant example of ancient natural native woodland. At the top of the brae a fence and stone dyke run uphill to the left. Follow this dyke - built to keep stock away from the steep sea cliffs - till it turns and runs parallel with the coastline.

For the next 1.5 km there is a 12 -15 metre wide grazed grassy sward between the dyke and the sloping cliff edge, providing a superb cliff-top walk, with good views of a nesting shag colony on sea rocks about a hundred metres north of the dyke corner, and the prospect of ravens and buzzards riding the up-draughts, and linnets and whinchats singing from bush and dyke. In winter, white mountain hares come down from the higher moors to forage and are easily distinguished from the common brown hare by their black-tipped white ears and partial white fur. Roe deer can be surprised from woodland edges, and perhaps a jack snipe, wintering from the Arctic, may be flushed to rise silently from a mud pool.

Further north, the grassy slopes widen and run down towards the rocks. However, walkers should continue along the top till just before the end of the cliff fence, then traverse down the slope to a kissing gate and march dyke close to Wilson's Burn. *Downanhill and Langdale Farms rely on electric fences to manage the pasture for their large dairy herd of Friesian cattle, and walkers should take great care not to touch the wires – or they might get a bit of a shock!*

Once across the burn, the field-edge Path follows the white-topped strainer posts of the electric fence that runs along the edge of the escarpment to another kissing gate, which short-cuts round the top of a very steep gully to a third gate. From here the Path runs north west over the blind shoulder of Downan Hill and down to join a new cattle track that the farmer has driven round the hillside. From here, there are fine views north across Ballantrae Bay to Ailsa Craig, and west towards Ireland. Leave this track at its closest point to a drystane dyke and follow the dyke eastwards to a kissing gate that opens on to the public road 100 metres north of Downanhill Cottage.

The road runs north through Langdale and Downan Farms, and as it approaches Kinniegar, walkers should be impressed by a huge 1.5 km-long gravel bank which is bisected by the mouth of the River Stinchar. This is a Site of Special Scientific Interest on account of its summer population of breeding terns - which should not be disturbed.

Before walkers give a fearful shudder when they read shortly about the violent 16th and 17th Century feuds of the Ardstinchar Kennedys, they should pause and look left over the fence as they approach Holm Park Farm. Jutting up from the roadside field can be seen the entrance shaft and ventilators of an underground nuclear fallout observation post - a relic of the 20th Century mega-feud between East and West - which was built in the 1950s at the beginning of the Cold War. In the event of a nuclear strike on Britain, this shelter would have been manned by a few local volunteer members of the Royal Observer Corps tasked to monitor the direction and extent of radio-active fallout. Though two or three observers inside might have been safe for a short while, what practical use this monitoring facility would have been to the survival of the rest of Ballantrae's - or Britain's - population is debatable!

Fishing on Stinchar

Passing the clachan of Garleffin, take great care when crossing the busy A77 (T) just south of the new bridge over the River Stinchar, and walk along the old road to the historic old Stinchar Bridge - which was built in 1776 from the stones of Ardstinchar Castle *(Gaelic ard = point)* whose louring ruins still strategically guard the mouth of the river. The Stinchar is a famous salmon river, and in summer and autumn when the water is low, people come from far and wide to lean over the old bridge parapet and gaze down into the deep sea pool, marvelling at the impressive sight of hundreds of fish leaping in frustration, or lying patiently in massed ranks, while waiting for autumn spates to take them up to their spawning grounds on gravel beds high in the Galloway uplands. With luck, they may even see a fly fisherman - with luck - cast, hook, play, and land a fine 'bar of silver'.

Bar of Silver being returned to the River Stinchar

Ardstinchar Castle was home to the Bargany branch of the Kennedy clan, and Mary Queen of Scots had an overnight stay here on 8 August 1563 - the last of several Banquet, Bed and Breakfast stops in Ayrshire's coastal castles - while undertaking her royal pilgrimage to Whithorn Priory. This Priory was founded on the site of *Candida Casa,* the first Celtic Christian church in Scotland, established by St Ninian around 400 AD - about 150 years before St Columba landed at Iona. Sometime later, towards the end of the 16th Century, the Bargany Kennedys were involved in a power struggle and bloody family feud with the Earl of Cassilis - over a woman and some land. The upshot was the death of Gilbert Kennedy the Laird of Bargany in a battle, and the murder of Sir Thomas Kennedy of Culzean - followed by several cover-up killings and the beheading of two murderers in 1611.

It is much more peaceful nowadays in the quiet village of Ballantrae, just round the corner.

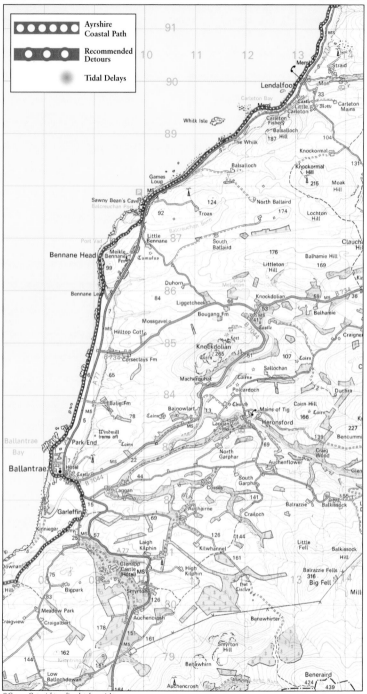

Ayrshire Coastal Path

Recommended Detours

Tidal Delays

2. BALLANTRAE Harbour - Bennane Head – Carleton Bay – Varyag Monument – LENDALFOOT

Distance = 10.5 km = 6.5 miles

Car Parks: The Vennel and Foreland, Ballantrae – Lendalfoot Hall

Walking Summary: *Moderate/Difficult* – pavements, sandy shore, old road, livestock, trunk road verge path – rocky beach.

Points of Interest:	
Transport:	Good hourly bus service
Historical:	Smugglers' Caves
	Sawney Bean legend
	Russian Cruiser *Varyag* monument
	Carleton Castle and motte
General:	Old fishing harbours
	Superb coastal scenery
Natural:	Cliff and shore breeding birds
	Diverse coastal flora
	Coastal geology
Eating/Provisions:	Ballantrae shop, Hotel and Garden Centre
Public Toilets:	Ballantrae - down The Vennel near recycling depot
Accommodation:	B&Bs and Hotel at Ballantrae
	(Check www.ayrshirecoastalpath.org)

The Village and Harbour: Ballantrae (population 293) is an ancient settlement. Formerly called Kirkcudbright-inner-Tig, after the old Church of St Cuthbert at the mouth of the Water of Tig, its name was changed at the beginning of the 17th Century, when a new church was built on the coast. The name is a clue to its antiquity, being an anglicised spelling of the Irish Gaelic *Bal-an-traigh* - which means 'the township by the beach'.

Many Galloway and Ayrshire place-names date from the 9th Century AD when Gaelic speaking *Gaidhels* from Ireland braved the short but dangerous crossing from Donaghadee to Portpatrick and invaded the south west, which became known as Galloway, the place of the Stranger Gaels. A similar invasion of the Irish *Scotti* tribe, taking the other obvious short route - from Antrim to the Mull of Kintyre - had already colonised the West Highlands in the 6th Century, creating the kingdom of Dalriada, and eventually giving Scotland its name, and two separate Gaelic speaking populations. Gaelic largely replaced the older Welsh Celtic tongue of the indigenous British tribes of Strathclyde, and the language of the Picts of the north. While Gaelic is still spoken in the Highlands, it had largely died out in the southwest by the end of the 16th Century. From the early 14th Century, Lowland Scots with its large Scandinavian vocabulary became the predominant language. Best known through the works of Robert Burns, the Mither Tongue is still widely spoken by Ayrshire folk, especially in the rural areas.

The small protected harbour at The Foreland to the north of the village dates from around 1846 when Ballantrae flourished as a fishing port due to the abundance of herring shoals spawning on the Ballantrae Bank which lies halfway to Ailsa Craig. In the old days, the scene would have been one of small herring smacks filling the small harbour, or setting their brown sails for the fishing banks. Once established, it became a port of call for a small steamer running between Stranraer and Glasgow. Later, with the onset of steam power, fishing boats became too large for the harbour and, as the stocks of herring declined, so did the fortunes of the village. However, many of the local boats in Girvan and Troon still carry a BA - Ballantrae registered number.

Ballantrae Harbour with Ailsa Craig and Bennane Head

Agriculture and forestry are now the only industries - apart from passing tourists on the busy A77, and salmon fishers and shooters on local estates. Young people who cannot get service jobs in local shops or hotels must travel to Girvan or Stranraer for work and - like so many other villages - a large proportion of the population is retired. The population has almost halved since 1951.

Walking: From the Stinchar bridge, follow the main road round to the church and branch left along down The Vennel to the beach. To the south are huge gravel banks, washed down the Stinchar over thousands of years by heavy spates. The river's tortuous struggle to reach the sea over a shallow bar is marked by a number of dead-end lagoons created where it has yielded to the power of the sea and shifting gravel tossed up by ferocious winter storms. *The gravel spit itself is a nature reserve for breeding terns, and should not be walked upon during the breeding season, for fear of crushing eggs or chicks underfoot.* To the north of the gravel bank lies a sandy beach which leads to the Ballantrae harbour, and is strewn along the high tide mark with driftwood and tree trunks washed down the Stinchar.

From Ballantrae, the Path leads north along a sandy shoreline for three kilometres past two cottages at Bennane Lea to a small cairn commemorating Henry Ewing Torbet, better known as 'Snib', a former Dundee bank clerk, who lived a hermit's life in nearby Bennane Cave till he died in 1983 at the age of seventy one. This deep cave has a walled frontage with a small door, beyond which is a large chamber at the back of which can dimly be seen another dividing wall with a door leading deep into the hillside. The floor is dry but deeply covered in pigeon droppings and the detritus of untidy visitors over the years. The walled frontage was apparently built to contain a blacksmith's smiddy when the road was being blasted and built round Bennane Head.

Beyond the cairn is the first of several kissing gates as the Path follows the old disused A77 road round Bennane Head and traverses gently up the hillside through several kissing gates to the Public Car park overlooking Balcreuchan Port and Sawney Bean's Cave, thus avoiding the new fast uphill section of the A77 on the landward side of Bennane Hill. *Since there are always a lot of sheep and cattle on this section, walkers should exercise due care, and avoid bringing dogs at any time.*

Cormorants, Shags and Ailsa Craig

In spring, fulmars and ravens nest on the Bennane cliffs, and buzzards and peregrines may also be seen hunting. The road margins are a mass of red campion and yellow gorse, and the hillside greenery is patch-worked with the white blossom of blackthorn and hawthorn. From the car park, wonderful views can be obtained of the Antrim coast, Ailsa Craig, Kintyre, and Arran, a view that changes dramatically with every day's walk north along the Ayrshire Coastal Path.

The OS map of this section of the coast from Ballantrae to Girvan shows several large named cliff-caves, used as travellers' shelters and smugglers' hideaways over the centuries. Attractive and romantic as they may appear on paper, all walkers tempted to pay them a visit should be warned that they do so at their own risk, as the approach paths or cave interiors could be dangerous. In fact, the owner of the Bennane Caravan Park, and the land on which Sawney Bean's Cave is situated, is against anyone visiting this site on grounds of possible liability problems.

The bloodcurdling tale of Sawney Bean and his family of cannibals living in a cave at Bennane Head, waylaying and eating poor benighted travellers at the end of the 16th Century - in the reign of James VI and during the time of the Kennedy Feuds - must have struck terror into the heart of anyone journeying through the wilds of Carrick. Not only would they have to run the gauntlet of the fearsome Kennedys - they would have to face the awful prospect of being eaten by the Beans!

And what a prospect, had only the tale been true - but never let the truth get in the way of a good tabloid story!

The horrible tales of a tribe of cannibal Beans terrorising coastal Carrick for twenty five years, of travellers disappearing into thin air, and of severed arms and legs found washed up on the coastline, finally led to King James himself leading a body of four hundred troops from Edinburgh to Galloway to search for the murderers. Bloodhounds led the king to the cannibals' cave, the mouth of which was flooded and concealed at high tide. Carrying torches the soldiers penetrated a mile long cave system to emerge into the main chamber where the Beans were trapped, surrounded by stacks of human limbs and bones lining the cave walls, along with heaps of gold, silver, watches, and weapons belonging to their victims. The Beans were arrested and marched to trial in Edinburgh, where the king personally sentenced all the men to be dismembered while alive, then burnt to death along with the women.

The tale is gruesome in the extreme, in the best tabloid press tradition, and like so many tabloid tales, contains *not a shred of truth*. No supporting evidence has ever been found in the Royal records, criminal trial records of the time, or the detailed burgh records of Edinburgh. Researchers over the years have concluded that the Sawney Bean story had its origins in sensational broadsheets dating from the 1730s, which gave their reading public gory details of executions and murders. Captain Armstrong's detailed map of Ayrshire published in 1775 does not show the cave. In fact, it only appears on Ordnance Survey maps from the 1970s onwards, when a local myth about the cave at Balcreuchan Port gained credence with the OS, and thus perpetuated the fallacy.

So that's the truth about Sawney Bean!

While somewhat noisier than the old Bennane road, the broad grass verge allows a good route northwards running downhill from the car park for 1.5 km - keeping between the fence and the seaward side of the crash barrier lining the west side of the A77 - to the entrance of the Caravan Park. This is much safer than the narrow roadside pavement which must be used for a short distance beyond the Park entrance, and from which it is advisable to clamber down and walk along the shoreline between the road and the sea as soon as practicable. *Fast vehicles will be passing close by on the same side and great care should be taken.*

Along the high water mark, the going is fairly rough in some places - a mixture of shingle, sand, and rocks - but at lower states of the tide, the inter-tidal sand is firm and provides easy walking for most of the way.

N.B. *In May and June, especially, it is extremely important on these narrow compressed coastal strips for walkers to walk on the sand below the tide-line where possible, and try to avoid tramping on patches of shingle above high water mark. This precaution is to minimise the high risk of standing on the nests of oystercatchers and ringed plovers, whose camouflaged clutches of speckled eggs on gravel are almost invisible.*

Oystercatcher chick or is it a stone!

Even more distressing is the prospect of squashing a tiny ringed plover chick - no bigger than a cotton reel - as it lies perfectly still and invisible among the pebbles hoping the danger will pass. It has happened! Many oystercatchers, ringed plovers and some common sandpipers, nest along the gravel beaches of the Ayrshire coast; *and an observant walker should see the hen bird quietly running, head low, down the beach away from its nesting area.* This should alert people that there is a nest close by - and to take avoiding action - long before the parent birds begin their anxious and frantic calling as they fly overhead, or run around feigning a broken wing to lead the predator away from their young. *Young wading birds leave the nest shortly after they hatch, and could be scattered and hiding over a wide area of gravel* - so great care must be taken to avoid harming them.

About two kilometres short of Lendalfoot, is the start of a spectacular collection of huge rocky outcrops, graphically described from its northern approach, beyond Lendalfoot, on Captain Armstrong's 1775 map of Ayrshire: '*At this Point between the Road & the Sea are two remarkable Rocks in the shape of Men and called the Old Laird & the Young, and for some Miles South the Road leads through sharp pointed Pyramids of rock standing on end which may be called a Forest of Stones instead of Trees.*'

Snugly nestled in the shelter provided by these strange outcrops of volcanic rock is a very pretty group of small wooden summerhouses with attractive and well-maintained gardens, which were built before the Second World War. For walkers who do not wish to scramble along the shore at this point, there is now the choice of a roadside footpath along to the wee village of Lendalfoot.

Varyag Memorial and Lendalfoot

On the promontory to the south of Carleton Bay is a picnic area now dominated by an impressive bronze memorial, which commemorates – not a British - but a Russian heroic naval encounter. Carleton Bay is the last resting place of the state-of-the-art, first rank, Imperial Russian battle-cruiser *Varyag*, which in 1904 was involved in an epic battle with six Japanese cruisers and seven destroyers during the Russo-Japanese War. Blockaded in a Korean port, hugely outgunned and outnumbered, the seamen of the *Varyag* refused to surrender, and finally scuttled their battered ship to prevent it falling into the hands of the enemy. The following year, the Japanese raised the ship and incorporated her into their own fleet as the *Soya*. In 1916, the Russians bought her back, and in 1917 sent her to Britain and the Clyde for a refit. Unfortunately, the Bolshevik Revolution and subsequent Civil War left the *Varyag* stranded in Britain and while she was being towed south for scrap in 1920, she ran aground and foundered 500 metres off Carleton Bay.

For Russians, the legendary heroism of the crew of the *Varyag* has a status akin to that of Nelson's crew on *HMS Victory* to the British; so in September 2007, the Varyag Monument was unveiled by the Russian Ambassador to Britain, while a Russian destroyer offshore laid a wreath - and the whole ceremony was televised live throughout the Russian Federation.

By the roadside beyond the monument is a neat row of fishermen's cottages - Carleton Fishery - built in 1832. On the shore is a small port with a sandy bottom and a breakwater on its west side, laboriously constructed by hand from large boulders cleared away from the seabed. On its northern side is an old black-tarred fisherman's hut, which has stood the test of time and tempest and adds to the atmosphere of Carleton Bay. Only two small rowing boats now remain - where a hundred years ago there would have been half a dozen brown-sailed sturdy vessels capable of a long day's fishing for herring on the Ballantrae Bank. From here, walkers might find it more pleasant to continue along a sandy beach edged with white bladder campion and a backdrop of tall, pale yellow sea kale.

Lendalfoot (population 120). Overlooking the village, 0.5 km along the hill road to Colmonell are the ruins of Carleton Castle, a tower house that was once the ancestral home of the Cathcarts - allies of the Bargany Kennedys. On the opposite side of the road lies a much earlier fortification, a motte - probably walled with wooden palisades - and dating from the 11-12th Century, just after the Norman Conquest.

This was a violent time, when the early Kings of Scotland found themselves in a precarious position; struggling simultaneously against the Lords of Galloway, the Lords of the Isles, and the Vikings; and to strengthen their power base, they encouraged a crowd of Norman barons - medieval 'heavies' - to come north, with the promise of grants of land in exchange for loyal support. Among them were the forebears of Robert the Bruce, the Stewart Dynasty, and many of today's Scottish landed aristocracy.

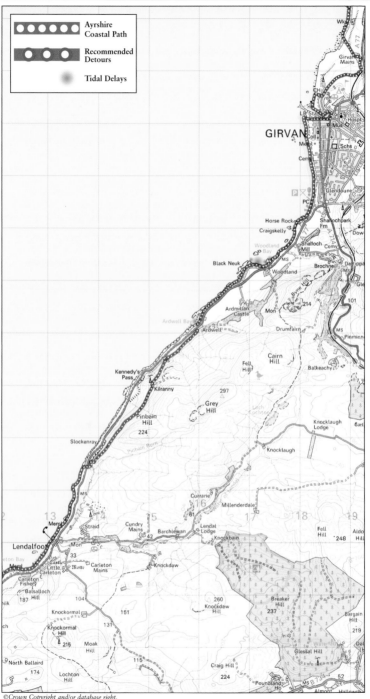

Ayrshire
Coastal Path

Recommended
Detours

Tidal Delays

GIRVAN

Wk

Girvan
Mains

A77

LB Sta
Hospl
Mus
Meml
Schs
Cem

Glendoune

PC

Horse Rock
Craigskelly
Shallochpark
Fm
Shalloch
Mill
Cemy
Dow

Woodland
Bay
MS
Black Neuk
Woodland
Brochneil
Darippa
Gle

Byne Hill
214
101
Ardmillan
Castle
Mon
Ardwell
Drumfairn
MS
Pinminn

Cairn
Hill
Fell
Hill
Balkeachy

Kennedy's
Pass
Kilranny
297
Grey
Hill
Loch
Lochton

Pinbain
Hill
224
Knocklaugh
Lodge
Earl

Slockenray
Pinbain Burn
Knocklaugh

MS
Currarie
16
61
Millenderdale
17
18
19

13
14
15
Cundry
Mains
Barchlewan
Lendal
Lodge
Knockbain
Fell
Hill
248
Aldo
Hill

Meml
Straid
Mon
42

Lendalfoot
33
Castle
Little
Motte
Carleton
Mains
Knockdaw
Knockdaw

Meul
Carleton
Fishery
Carleton
Balsalloch
Hill
187
104
260
Knockdaw
Hill
Breaker
Hill
237
Bargain
Hill
219

Knockormal
151
Waterhead
Da

Knockormal
Hill
215
131
Moak
Hill
Glessal Hill

North Ballaird
174
Lochton
Hill
115
Craig Hill
224
Poundland
Ho
MS
B734
52
Almont
Hallow

3. LENDALFOOT - Pinbain Hill - Old coach road above Kennedy's Pass - Ardwell - Ardwell Bay - Woodland Bay - Girvan Promenade – GIRVAN

8/10/10

Distance = 10.5 km = 6.5 miles

Car Parks: **Lendalfoot Hall – Girvan Promenade or Harbour**

Walking Summary: *Moderate/Difficult* – sand and rocky outcrops, 100m ascent on old coach road, livestock, farm track, rocky shore, trunk road pavement, promenade.

Points of Interest:	
Transport:	Good hourly bus service
Historical:	Shipwreck memorial Penbain Hill 18th century coach road
General:	Ailsa Craig High-level panoramas of Firth of Clyde
Nature:	Seabirds, Seals, coastal and upland flora Coastal Geology
Eating/Provisions:	Girvan Town Centre Restaurants Woodlands Farm Shop
Public toilets:	Girvan - Ainslie Park Harbour point - next to Swimming Pool
Accommodation:	B&Bs, Girvan Hotels and Guesthouses Ardmillan Castle Caravan and Campsite Town centre - Strathavon Caravan and Campsite (Check www.ayrshirecoastalpath.org)

Walking: The walk - a mixture of firm sand, small beach pebbles, and rock outcrops - continues along the shore from Lendalfoot. A few hundred metres north of the village, protected by a small white-walled enclosure - and contrasting with the monolithic grandeur of that of the *Varyag* - is a simple modest memorial to a shipwrecked crew washed up on this rugged coast almost three hundred years ago. The poignant message reads: '*Erected to the memory of Archibald Hamilton and crew, natives of King's Cross, Arran, who were drowned near this spot in December 1711.*

> *Ye passengers whoe'er ye are*
> *As ye pass on this way*
> *Disturb ye not this small respect*
> *That's paid to sailors' clay'*

For the next 1.5 km, the shore walk continues on a mixture of rocks, shingle, and sand till the Pinbain Burn is reached and the main road leaves the flat raised beach and become squeezed between the hills and the sea at Kennedy's Pass. Walkers are advised to continue along the shore, or keep well over to the left of the grassy roadside verge till past the 'Reduce speed now' notice, which is just before a dangerous right hand bend. When opposite the gate leading into a quarry-like hollow, **cross the A77 (T) very carefully** and go through the kissing gate. In May and June there are several pairs of fulmars nesting on the cliff to the left of the rough track that ascends sharply on to the hillside. From here it is easy to look down on the nests with binoculars, and from the top of the slope looking south, walkers will also see a magnificent example of one of the classic Ayrshire raised beaches left after the last Ice Age, where it is quite easy to imagine great seas surging against the base of the escarpments.

Start of Kennedy's Pass and Pinbain Hill

The farmer at Ardwell has no objections to walkers using the old coach road, but asks for care during the lambing season - April to early May - when the sheltered hillside field on the southern approach to the coach road holds lambing ewes. In the past his ewes have been startled and separated from their lambs at a vulnerable stage. Walkers should not take dogs over this section.

Walkers are now on the old 18th century coach road, built around 1780, which rises and traverses the slopes of Pinbain Hill for 2 km, bypassing the rocky perils of Kennedy's Pass. Nowadays it avoids the noisy traffic of the modern road - and what would otherwise be a dangerous and unpleasant stretch of verge walking. The present road through the pass was only built after motorcars took over from horse drawn vehicles. As you walk along the level top section, look closely at the road surface, which still shows areas of the original cambered, 'macadamised' type of surface pioneered in the late 18th Century by John Loudon McAdam (born in Ayr) – a technique that revolutionised road-building throughout Britain.

While most people think of 'Tarmacadam' as John McAdam's invention - although by coincidence he did in fact develop one of the first coal-tar extraction plants at Muirkirk in upland Ayrshire to provide tar for Nelson's ships - he did not himself make the later connection between coal tar and stone chips.

McAdam's great invention was the use of carefully graded stone for the road surface, broken into pieces no more that 1.5 inches (40mm) in diameter, which, when laid as a cambered surface, became impacted and jammed against each other to form a stable, smooth and durable surface.

The traverse along Pinbain Hill is well worth the effort for its marvellous high-level perspective of the Firth of Clyde. When standing on the tide line, a man's visible horizon is only three miles (5 Km), but from one hundred metres above sea level, it is possible to see large ships far out to sea that would have been invisible from the shore. The sight of a buzzard being mobbed by a family of ravens, and a glimpse of a fast moving peregrine can add pleasure to the view.

18th Century Coach Road above Kennedy's Pass

Botanically, at this height there are subtle changes in the flora. The vibrant yellow of flag iris and birds-foot trefoil abound as on the shore, but on the hillside, moor grasses and bog cotton are evident, and on the wet banks of the roadside ditches, the lime-coloured, midge-spotted, star-shaped basal leaves and blue flowers of the insectivorous butterwort can be found, along with the more innocuous mayflower. The geology of this area is also very special and often the subject of study by parties of geologists searching for rare green serpentine.

Winter Gale at Kennedy's Pass

Opposite Kennedy's Pass, Ailsa Craig is at its closest point to the Ayrshire Coast - 13.5 km or 8.5 miles. Situated halfway between Glasgow and Belfast, this huge cake-shaped rock rising 338 metres (1110 ft) above sea level is an impressive landmark viewed from anywhere in the Firth of Clyde. Halfway between Glasgow and Belfast, it was affectionately dubbed 'Paddy's Milestone' by the thousands of Irish who used to migrate back and forth by steamer between Scotland and Northern Ireland.

Formed largely of igneous rock - granite, and basalt columns similar to those found on the Giant's Causeway in Antrim, and the Hebridean Isle of Staffa - it is the plug of an ancient volcano whose soft rock sides have been eroded away over millions of years. For well over a hundred years, its fine micro-granite has been quarried for curling stones. Granite boulders are still shipped to Girvan by boat and transported to the small Ayrshire village of Mauchline, the site of the only curling stone factory in the world. The ancient game of curling - 'the roaring game' - has been played on the ice of Scottish lochs for over 450 years, and recently gained unprecedented worldwide recognition when it became an official sport in the 2002 Winter Olympics. The Gold Medal winning all-Scottish British women's rink included two Ayrshire lasses, and all the curling stones were of granite from Ailsa Craig. Despite the burgeoning popularity of the sport worldwide since the 2002 Olympics, there is little likelihood of the Craig disappearing entirely due to world demand for curling stones!

Which is lucky for the gannets! With binoculars it should be possible to see the great bird cliffs on which 15,000 pairs of gannets breed, along with thousands of guillemots, razorbills, kittiwakes, shags and cormorants. Thousands of puffins also used to breed on the Craig till they were wiped out by rats - probably landed from ships - which, once established on an island with no natural predators, began to decimate the bird population by eating their eggs and small young. A curiosity on the island is the presence of a healthy population of slowworms - snakelike legless lizards which can sometimes be surprised by walkers, basking in the sun on the path to the summit. Just how did they get there? Are they relics of the last Ice Age?

Ailsa Craig from Ardwell Bay

About twenty years ago, a team of naturalists from Glasgow University began a systematic programme of setting down rat poison in burrows and crevices all over the island. In this they were aided by Royal Navy Sea King helicopters from HMS Gannet at Prestwick, which over several years flew in five tons of the stuff! The campaign paid off, and now Ailsa

Craig is rat-free and the first puffins have started to return. In 2006 there were 30 breeding pairs, but it will take many, many years for a large colony to re-establish itself. Gannets on the other hand can often be seen fishing close inshore on this stretch of coastline. Large, pure white birds with black wing tips and a five foot wingspan, they soar high above the water before diving like darts, wings closing at the last moment, to catch and swallow their prey deep beneath the surface.

Close by the old shepherd's cottage of Kilranny is the second of two radio repeater masts on the hillside. The old cottage area has been converted into a sheep fank, and to avoid any disturbance, the Path lead through two kissing gates round the seaward side of the building to rejoin the road beyond it. It is interesting to speculate on the origin of this old house, standing as it does at the head of a steep brae. While it may have finished up as a shepherd's cottage, it probably started life as a toll house or a roadsman's dwelling on the turnpike road - the roadsman's task being to break stones, clear ditches, and maintain his section of track to the set standards of the Turnpike trustees. A pair of trace horses may even have been stabled here to assist the mail-coach horses to draw their coach up the steep ascent from Ardwell.

Now walkers will descend this steep road northwards towards the shore. At the bottom, the Path runs along a rough farm track at the base of the escarpment - or the top of the old raised beach - to the farm of Ardwell, and rejoins the main road just before the first of the farm steadings.

Walkers should be aware that in the summer months, the farmer may occasionally have a couple of beef bulls grazing this low ground for a few weeks along with the cattle while the upper pastures are rested. These bulls are generally docile when with their cows, but it is the ultimate responsibility of walkers to make their own safety assessment and judgment, and if unsure, they should either keep very close to the roadside fence and be ready for a quick jump – or risk crossing the busy A77 (T) at the foot of the hill and then clamber along the rough shore as best they can till better shore walking is reached at Ardwell!

When using the farm track, pass through the final kissing gate by the farm and carefully cross the A77 (T) to its shore side. Form here walkers can clamber down over rock slabs on to the shore, but if the tide is fully in they may have to walk along the grass verge well clear of the road for a short distance till beyond the farm, then join the beach - which is a mixture of rock, shingle and firm sand from here to Girvan. A kilometre to the northeast lie the ruins of Ardmillan Castle, another old Kennedy stronghold. If desired, there is a section of old road between Ardmillan and Black Neuk that can be used for easier walking. Beyond the Black Neuk, a roadside pavement runs past Woodland for the final kilometre to Girvan - though the beach remains comfortable and pleasant walking. If using this pavement, walkers will find that there is one dangerous bend where there is no footway or verge for 130 metres. Here they should descend on to the beach again, just before they reach the small burn running under the road 200 m short of Shalloch Mill.

Girvan from Black Neuk

About 80 m beyond Shalloch Mill, cut up on to the bank and follow the beach and path round the seaward side of Ainslie Manor Nursing Home. This is more pleasant than walking along the narrow pavement next to traffic on the main road. Just beyond, is a small section of pavement leading to the car park at Ainslie Park.

From here on it is a pleasant stroll along the promenade to Girvan harbour, and the Town Centre can be accessed easily by following any of the small streets running inland from the prom and Stair Park.

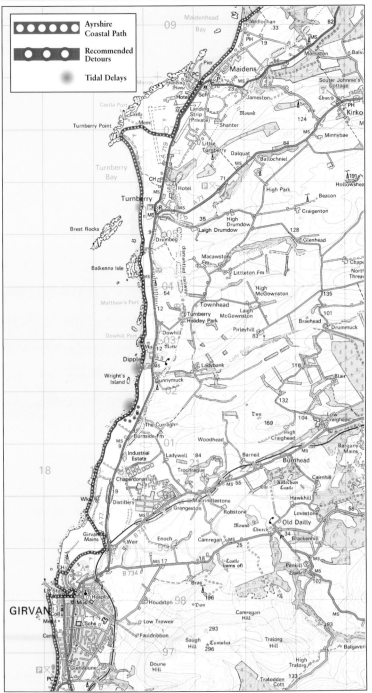

Ayrshire
Coastal Path

Recommended
Detours

Tidal Delays

17/2/11

4. GIRVAN Town Centre - Harbour Road Bridge – Harbour Point - Golf Course Road - Girvan Mains - Chapeldonan - Dipple Shore - TURNBERRY - Turnberry Bay - Turnberry Golf Course - A719 road - MAIDENS

Distance = 13.0 km = 8.1 miles

Car Parks: **Girvan Harbour - Turnberry Post Office - Maidens Green**

Walking Summary: *Moderate/Difficult* – pavements, minor road, farm track and wrack roads, livestock, rough gravel and sandy shore. Three short Tidal Stretches.

Points of Interest:	
Transport:	Trains from Ayr and Stranraer Good hourly bus service
Historical:	Roman Camp at Girvan Main Dowhill Motte Turnberry Castle - birthplace of Robert the Bruce Turnberry Lighthouse RAF Memorial at Turnberry
General:	Ailsa Craig Alginate Factory Grant's Whisky distillery Coastal agriculture Turnberry Hotel and Open Championship golf course
Nature:	Seabirds off Dipple Shore and Turnberry Point Glacial boulders on shoreline
Eating/provisions:	Girvan Town Centre shops, pubs and restaurants Dowhill Farm Restaurant and Shop Balkenna Tearoom Turnberry and Maidens Stores and PO
Car Parking:	Girvan harbour Turnberry Post Office Maidens Bay
Public toilets:	Girvan - next to swimming pool at Harbour Point Beside Turnberry Post Office Maidens Harbour
Accommodation:	B&Bs Girvan Hotels and Guesthouses Girvan Caravan and Campsite Turnberry and Maidens hotels and B&Bs (Check www.ayrshirecoastalpath.org)

Girvan Harbour

The Town and Harbour: The River Girvan may have derived its name from the Gaelic *Garbh Abhain* - meaning 'rough river' - as did the settlement at its mouth, which grew and prospered to become the pleasant, compact small fishing and tourist town of **Girvan** (population 6992). Like so many of the other Clyde coastal resorts, Girvan had its heyday in the years before and after the Second World War; before large airliners swept city folk off to foreign holiday resorts; and large fishing boats swept the Clyde clean of herring and cod.

Girvan's streets, promenade and beach still throng with day and weekend tourists during the summer, but few families will now spend their traditional fortnight's holiday by a Scottish seaside. In the harbour, the fishing fleet is much smaller, and boats now fish mainly for prawns and scallops, with random other species taken as by-catch. A few herring are still taken, but stocks have never recovered despite a total fishing ban lasting many years.

First mentioned in a report of 1683, the harbour in early times was basically a river creek, into which small open fishing boats, and half-decked sailing vessels from Ireland and the Highlands could only venture at high tide. Despite this, Girvan prospered and grew from the profits of widespread smuggling as well as legitimate coastal trade - and from a glut of herring in the 1760s - but it was not until 1847 that it was improved sufficiently to take vessels up to 10 feet draught, and enlarged to accommodate a fishing-fleet of 34 boats. Today's harbour has a much better protected entrance, though the harbour bar can still cause problems. Noble's Shipyard is one of only a few small shipyards remaining on the Clyde. Although it has few new builds nowadays, it is kept busy servicing RNLI lifeboats, and repairing fishing boats from as far away as the north east of Scotland. Girvan Lifeboat is stationed here, and the pontoon is always busy with local and visiting yachts.

Open boats carrying up to twelve passengers sail from this pontoon during the summer on sea-fishing trips - or day excursions to Ailsa Craig with a landing for three hours - weather and tides permitting.

Grant's Distillery, and the ISP Alginates factory are two of the town's main employers, and agriculture is still plays a very important part in the local economy. As for the future, there are at present, ambitious plans by Girvan Community Development Ltd (GCDL) supported by the RSPB, to build the Ailsa Craig Centre, which will provide a live link between Ailsa Craig and Girvan, whereby tourists and school parties will be able to experience Ailsa Craig and its magnificent seabird colonies by means of live TV cameras on the island.

Walking: Walk along from the harbour to the town centre traffic lights, turn left and follow the main road. Girvan Tourist Office lies about 150 m north of the town centre on the right-hand side of the road. On the seaward side at this point, turn left and follow signs for the golf course and caravan park. Crossing the road bridge over the River Girvan, bear left down past Noble's Shipyard and onwards to the Coastguard Station. From here follow the path along the harbour-side past the old derelict coal quay, which has been transformed by the Rotary Club of Girvan into a fine viewpoint and garden, as their Centenary Project to commemorate one hundred years of Rotary International. Follow the Path as it swings right along the shore between the breakwaters and a broad green in front of a terrace of houses.

Cross the green by the Starter's Hut for Girvan's Municipal Golf Course and walk through a gap in the terrace down a short road leading on to Golf Course Road. This is a pleasant quiet road running north alongside the River Girvan and bisecting the Golf Course. To the east are fine views of the fertile farmlands and wooded rolling hills of the Girvan Valley – and of course Wm Grant and Son's Distillery. At the north end of Golf Course Road lies Girvan Mains Farm. It was here during the very hot summer of 1976, just a few metres west of the road and a hundred metres south of this very fertile farm, that aerial photography revealed the crop-marked outline of a Roman marching camp. Very little major evidence of Roman occupation had previously been found in Ayrshire, apart from the Roman camp at Loudoun Hill near the Lanarkshire border.

On the seaward side of Girvan Mains, massive reinforced sea defences beyond the boundary wall protect valuable farmland from the forces of nature. Several years ago, when heavy erosion was threatening to wash away many acres of this fine alluvial soil, a huge coastal protection project was undertaken, resulting in 500 m of armoured sea wall that effectively and unfortunately forms a barrier to walking along this stretch of shore at high tide. The inter-tidal shore area round the point is also crowded with large round granite bounders, which are difficult to negotiate when the tide is out.

Consequently, to avoid any risk of sprained ankles or worse, the Coastal Path has chosen this short interesting inland detour, which takes advantage of a right of way running through the farm courtyard.

Walkers should remember that Girvan Mains is a very busy, large working farm, and great care should be taken to avoid farm machinery and disturbance to livestock. Please pass through the courtyard quickly and quietly. Beyond the courtyard is a 300-metre track leading towards the shore, which passes two cottages – and Gallow Hill on the right. On this low hill in olden times, the Kennedys and their ilk would mete out justice as they saw it, to the poor miscreants of Girvan.

Running parallel to the shore from Girvan to Turnberry - on the raised beaches left when land rose after the last Ice Age - are the famous, frost-free fields of fine light rich soil in which the unsurpassable, delicious 'Early Ayrshire' tatties have been grown for over a hundred years. These early Epicures are planted in mid February, and in most years will survive to be harvested in May and June. Despite 'new potatoes' being imported from Jersey, Cyprus and Egypt, and available most of the year in supermarkets, none can ever match the mouth-watering flavour of our own Early Ayrshires - eaten with a wee knob of butter!

Winter wrack near Girvan

The cart track runs along the shore and makes for easy walking past the new waterworks to the water-filled sandstone quarries at Chapeldonan, which are pumped to irrigate the potato fields. It was originally called a 'wrack road' - one of many along the coast used by local farmers for over two centuries to cart tons of seaweed from the beach to fertilise their fields. Beyond the quarries it continues along the foreshore grass through an summer avenue of sweet-scented, white Burnet roses till it reaches two cottages bordering the beach, which are fronted by a high, protective, armoured sea wall.

Burnet Roses on Dipple Shore

N.B. *The regular Path route continues along the foreshore below the cottages at most states of the tide, but on many days each month for 2-3 hours either side of all high tides, the shore at this point may be impassable.*

Though a farm track leads up from the shore in front of the first row of houses, in order to preserve their privacy, *an alternative route should be taken at high tide along a field edge path* accessed through a kissing gate 200 m south of the first cottage. From here the narrow field-edge path runs for 500m behind both sets of houses and through several kissing gates to rejoin the beach 200m north of the last cottage. *Walkers should take care not to trample or damage crops when using this escape route path.*

Between Curragh cottages and the Dipple Burn, the beach is a mixture of sand and shingle. *Except for a 1-2 hour spell either side of high spring tides* - it is possible to cross the mouth of the Dipple Burn and walk along the shore past the unique Alginates Factory. To assist walkers, a concrete causeway-ford has been built at the high water mark, which should allow them to splash across without taking their boots off - unless confronted by a very high tide or spate.

Causeway at Dipple Burn

Dipple Shore

At any high water level greater than 2.7 m (Ayr) or during a spate, walkers may be forced to wait or wade, or detour at their own risk up the wrack road on the south side of the burn past the cottages and along the grass verge bordering the Factory on the busy main road, to rejoin the path further along down a wrack road opposite Dowhill Farm. This is a dangerous stretch of road and not recommended, and great care should be taken with the heavy traffic.

Widely known locally as the 'Seaweed Factory', the Alginate Factory was built during World War II when the government was looking for materials to replace jute and balsa wood, and thought that calcium alginate would provide a substitute. A use was found for alginates in making camouflage netting.

Brown seaweeds containing natural alginates are harvested from cold water regions of the world. Imported from Ireland, Iceland, and as far away as Tasmania as a dried, powdered meal, ISP Alginates use several hundred tonnes per week in their processing plant. Sodium and calcium alginates are used as thickeners, stabilisers and gelling agents in hundreds of day-to-day food products – ice creams, desserts, salad dressings, beer; also in slow release medicines, cosmetics, and the printing industry

Opposite Dowhill Farm, with its excellent farm shop and restaurant, an access track leads to and from the beach to the A77 road. On the hilltop behind Dowhill can be seen a prominent motte or hill fort, possibly dating from the lawless days of the Lords of Galloway, who ruled this region independent of the King of Scotland, in the early 12th Century after the Norman Conquest. The motte is difficult to access through brambles, but the determined walker will find a central mound edged by an earth rampart, and surrounded by a ditch and second rampart. When in use, both sets of ramparts would have been topped by wooden palisades, with wooden living quarters constructed on the mound within the inner palisade

Along part of this stretch of shore, especially at high tide, walking might be easier if a path was trodden along the grassy bank on the shore side of the field boundary fence, as the beach is mainly shingle, and the walking a little harder.

Below high water mark is an interesting area of old red sandstone slabs on which are perched a collection of large round granite boulders, possibly glacial erratics from the Galloway Hills or Ailsa Craig. The Dipple shore is a favourite haunt for bird-watchers, especially in the autumn and winter months when wintering seabirds and passage migrants can be seen both along the strand and offshore. *In spring and summer, great care should be taken to avoid disturbing nesting ringed plovers and oystercatchers, or tramping on nests and young fledglings. If possible walk below the high water mark and away from shingle patches.*

As the walk proceeds north along firm sand it fords a small shallow burn by an old fisherman's hut. A few hundred metres further on is the mouth of the larger Milton Burn at Turnberry, where another helpful causeway-ford has been laid to assist walkers to cross the burn without taking their boots off. Here a popular beach access path leads inland along the southern boundary of Turnberry Golf Course to the A719 and the public car park at Turnberry Post Office.

N.B. When a big spate meets a high tide greater than 2.6 m (Ayr) backed-up water will submerge the weir, and walkers in either direction who have mistimed their arrival will either have to wait - or use their own discretion about following the burn upstream to the nearest bridge.

High spring tide impassable at Milton Burn

Milton Burn at low tide

Walkers starting from the car park at Turnberry Post Office should turn right on the A719, walk up past the large white house on the shore side, go through the metal kissing gate beyond it, and down the access path to the mouth of the Milton Burn. From here it is a fine stroll along the firm sandy sweep of Turnberry Bay towards Turnberry Lighthouse and Castle. Just before the lighthouse sits one of the most famous, spectacular, and terrifying golf tees in the world - the 9th at Turnberry, known as 'Bruce's Castle' - from which Open Championship competitors have to drive over the sea to reach the fairway.

Before passing between 'Bruce's Castle' and the 8th green, walkers enjoying their day out are requested to respect the right of golfers to enjoy theirs, by observing basic golfing etiquette. Have the courtesy to stand still and quiet while someone is playing a shot or putting - keep a good lookout – and refrain from walking over the path if someone is about to play.

To avoid both a risk of serious injury to walkers from flying golf balls, and disturbance to golfers playing off the tee - the designated Coastal Path heads inland along the old wrack road from the beach which runs diagonally across part of the course, parallel to and between two fairways, till it reaches the remains of a wartime runway and then the lighthouse access road. At this point, anyone wishing to have a closer look at the Castle, the Lighthouse, or the RAF War Memorial, could walk with care back along the lighthouse access road - but it is not part of the Coastal Path.

They do so at their own peril, since they must cross the 9th fairway and run the risk being hit by golf balls. They must continue to remember basic golfing etiquette -` and should also retrace their steps and rejoin the walk where they left it.

It is possible with great care at low tide to walk along the shore, round the base of the rocks on which the ruins of Turnberry Castle sit, and penetrate the interior through two sea caves. Very little now remains of what must have been a great fortification - of a size to equal that of Dunure Castle further up the coast. A latrine chute opening on to the rocks is still visible on the seaward side; and Turnberry Lighthouse has been built on the moat at the southern part of the site.

Despite its sad appearance today as an insignificant ruin, Turnberry Castle played a major pivotal role in the course of Scottish history. It was here in 1273, that Marjorie, the recently widowed Countess of Carrick, came across the handsome young Robert Bruce, son of the Lord of Annandale, a claimant to the Scottish throne, who was hunting on her lands. Taking a fancy to him, she had him taken forcibly back to the castle, and pleasantly entertained him to the extent that they were married after a courtship of only a few days.

Their son Robert, who was almost certainly born at Turnberry in 1274, became in due course the Earl of Carrick, and eventually King Robert the Bruce. Having previously fled the Scottish mainland to escape from English persecution, it was from the island of Arran to Turnberry that Bruce sailed with three hundred men in 1307 to begin the great struggle for Scottish

Independence - full of high hopes on sighting smoke from what he thought was an agreed signal fire on a Carrick hill. It was a mistake - local peasants were burning whin bushes - and on landing near Turnberry, Bruce found the population cowed and not ready for an uprising. Undeterred, he slaughtered most of Turnberry Castle's English garrison, and then took to the wild hills of Ayrshire and Galloway to begin a long guerrilla campaign that culminated in victory at Bannockburn in 1314.

The present Earl of Carrick is HRH Prince Charles, Prince of Wales.

Turnberry Lighthouse was built in 1873 by David and Thomas Stevenson to protect shipping from the Brest Rocks - a large flat outcrop lying offshore about 2km due south of Turnberry Point which had seen many wrecks. The Light became automatic in 1986 and the keepers' houses now belong to Turnberry Hotel.

Turnberry Lighthouse

On a knowe near the Lighthouse stands the RAF War Memorial to a large number of young airmen who died flying from RAF Turnberry, a wartime fighter pilot training airfield. This monument is only accessible by crossing a fairway, and while there is no visible clearly marked access path, it is worth a visit.

Six miles out to sea, two thirds of the way across to Pladda Lighthouse, lies the wreck of U33, depth-charged and sunk by the minesweeper *HMS Gleaner* while sneaking into the Firth of Clyde to lay mines on 12 February 1940. Two of the rotor wheels from the submarine's Enigma coding machine were discovered in the pockets of a crewmember who had forgotten to throw them overboard. They were the first naval code wheels to fall into the hands of British Intelligence, and greatly helped in the famous efforts of the brilliant cryptographers at Bletchley Park to break the German codes.

After the fall of France in 1940, the North Western Approaches leading through the North Channel to the Clyde and Liverpool became Britain's main lifeline route for vital trans-Atlantic supply convoys. Huge efforts were made by German U-boats and bombers to disrupt this traffic - and even greater efforts were made by Royal Navy escort ships and Coastal Command aircraft to protect our merchant fleet and defeat the U-boat menace. The Clyde was the main disembarkation port for American GIs in the run-up to D-Day. The *Queen Mary* and *Queen Elizabeth* ran a fortnightly shuttle service between America and the Clyde, each carrying from 10-15,000 troops per trip. From 1942 to 1944, 339 troopships brought over 1,319,089 GIs into the Clyde; and in 1944, from the Clyde, 75,000 troops embarked for the invasion of North Africa.

Hundreds of ships were sunk in that narrowing gap between Tiree and Islay and the Irish coast, and thousands of men, women, and children perished in the icy waters. Unlike the young RAF fliers, they have no memorial. Please linger a while on those beautiful and tranquil views across the Firth to the Mull of Kintyre and the unforgiving cruel seas beyond, and humbly reflect on the brave young men and women of many nationalities who, passing that way for the last time, gave their lives for that freedom to live and roam and gaze, which we now take for granted. Let this be their memorial.

From the wrack road junction the Coastal Path now runs east along the Lighthouse road, which bisects the Open Championship Ailsa Course and joins the A719. Like the Hotel, this world-famous golf course was built over a hundred years ago, and both celebrated their Centenary in 1906. *Once again, walkers are expected to show courtesy to any golfers teeing off or playing across the access road, and should also exercise great care to avoid being struck by golf balls.* From this road can also be seen several of the old wartime runways from which young Spitfire pilots flew on training sorties; and to the right is a majestic view of the Hotel sitting in its red-roofed, five-starred splendour on the hillside. Once through the kissing gate at the road-end, turn left on the A719, and walk along the tarmac verge path that leads north to the village of Maidens; passing en route yet another of the old runways, part of which was once used occasionally by light aircraft flying to Turnberry Hotel.

Turnberry Hotel was built by the Glasgow and South Western Railway Company as the world's very first Golfing Hotel, and was serviced by the picturesque Dunure and Maidens Light Railway from Ayr, which cost £300,000 to construct (£20,000,000 in present-day money). Unfortunately, this extravagant Edwardian transport venture failed to anticipate the rise of the motor car - and the slump of the Great Depression. Sadly the railway only carried passenger traffic to Turnberry for 24 years until 1930. It reopened briefly in 1932 towards the end of

Turnberry Bay and Hotel and Wrack Road from beach

the Depression, but finally closed to passenger trains a year later in June 1933. However it continued to run for another thirty years as a freight line and carried the 'Potato Special' which was vital to local farmers in transporting their precious cargoes of early Ayrshire potatoes to the Glasgow market and on down into England.

N.B. During an Open Championship, or any other major golf championship being staged at Turnberry, this section of Coastal Path across the Ailsa Course will be closed temporarily to the general public by South Ayrshire Council, and walkers will have use the access path from the mouth of the Milton Burn up to the Post Office and then follow the A719 roadside pavement from Turnberry to Maidens.

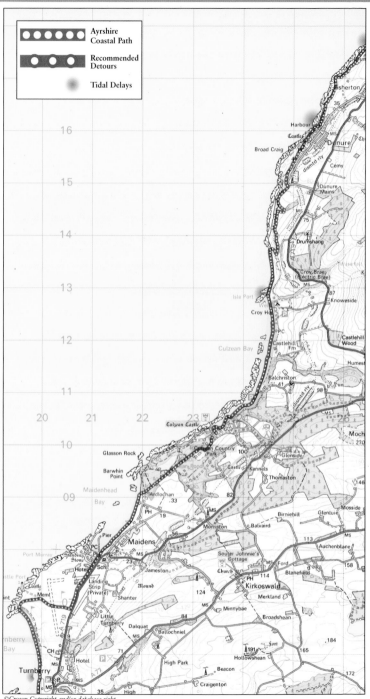

Ayrshire Coastal Path

Recommended Detours

Tidal Delays

25/2/11

5. MAIDENS Bay - Cliff Walk or Swan Pond and Walled Garden to CULZEAN CASTLE - Culzean Visitor Centre - Culzean (Croy) Bay - Old 18th Century shore road on Drumshang – Cliff top path - track down to DUNURE CASTLE (Kennedy Park)

Distance = 10.0 km = 6.2 miles

Car Parks: Maidens Green - Culzean Castle - Croy Bay - Kennedy Park, Dunure

Walking Summary: *Moderate/Difficult* – sandy beaches, park paths, rocky outcrops, field-edge paths, livestock. One short Tidal Stretch.

Points of Interest:	
Transport:	Good bus service
Historical:	Culzean Castle – Robert Adam jewel in the crown of the National Trust for Scotland, Eisenhower display (Open Apr-Oct) Coastline famous for smuggling in 18th Century Dunure Castle - one of a coastal line of Kennedy Clan castles Dunure Harbour - old port for a fleet of sail-driven herring boats
General:	Maidens Harbour Culzean Castle and Country Park, Swan Pond, gardens, deer park, woodland walks, Visitor Centre Croy Bay is popular picnic and bathing beach in summer. Dramatic views of Ailsa Craig, Ireland, Kintyre, and Arran.
Nature:	Specimen trees in Culzean Country Park Woodland and coastal birdlife Coastal geology. Raised beaches, agates, yellow sandstone cliffs with smugglers' caves
Eating/Provisions:	Maidens - Store and Restaurant Culzean Swan Pond Kiosk (limited opening in summer only) Culzean Country Park Visitor Centre Restaurant (100-1700 daily Apr-Oct ; limited winter opening) Dunure Shop and Inn
Public Toilets:	Maidens Harbour and Maidens Bay Culzean Country Park - Swan Pond, Deer Park Car Park (Apr-Oct), and Visitor Centre Croy Bay Car Park (Apr-Oct only) Dunure Castle - Kennedy Park
Accommodation:	Culzean Camping and Caravanning Club Site Dunure B&B Farm B&Bs (Check www.ayrshirecoastalpath.org)

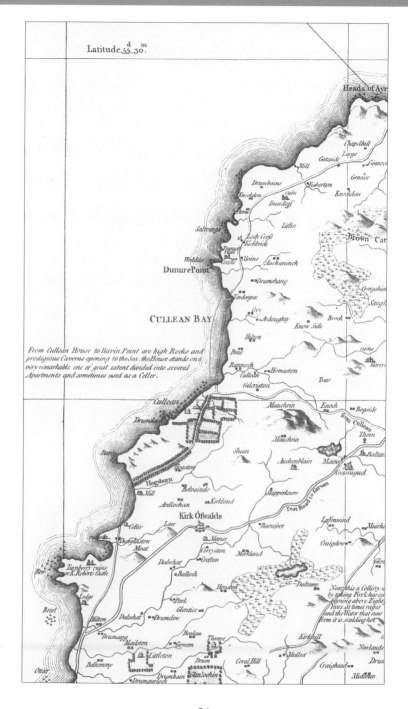

Latitude, 55,.30.

Heads of Ayr

Chapelhill

Largs

Gateside

Linnoe

Mill

Geneose

Drumbains

Fisherton

ruin

Knockdaw

Knockdon

Dundujj

Liffin

Carn

Saltpanse

Brown Car

Lady Cross

Kirkbride

Dunur

Pann

Auchaninch

Welda

Ruins

Wodda

Dunure Point

Drumshang

Crigshie

Saugh

Tinderyree

Iry

DUNURE POINT

CULLEAN BAY

Andoughty

Brock

Know Side

Hilton

From Cullean House to Bavin Point are high Rocks and
prodigious Caverns opening to the Sea, the House stands on a
very remarkable one of great extent divided into several
Apartments and sometimes used as a Celler.

Brae

ruins

Carry

Rannoch

Homeston

Cullean

Trees

Gilcriston

Cullean

Mauchrin

Enoch

Bogside

Drumst

from Cullean

Thorn

Mauchrin

Baltar

Shean

Auchenblain

Main

Barr

Crossinguel

Hogston

Skippaknow

Post Road to Girvan

Hogsburn

Belwinds

Kirkland

Ardlochan

Law

KIRK OSWALDS

Burnfoot

Laffenwind

Muirh

Celler

Manse

Craigdew

Douglaston

Kew

Moat

Corryston

Mayland

Turnberry ruins
or K. Roberts Castle

Dalwhat

Grofton

Daltamy

Lodge

Balloch

Near this a Colliery n
by taking Fire Chas con
burning above Eight
Years at times ridges
and the Water that runs
from it is scalding hot

Brest

Park

Houston

Glentice

Otter

Milton

Dalwhat

Drumdow

Kirkhill

Newlands

Drumsegg

Beakan

Thrne

Mailston

Gowan

Drum

Coral Hill

Midlex

Craighead

Midtoun

Belhemmy

Littleton

Drum

Drumbain

Glenlochin

Drumanuroch

Walking: Maidens (population 471) is a small fishing village, though the picturesque drying harbour, sheltered behind a series of natural outcrops called the Maidenhead Rocks, is now mainly a haven for pleasure craft. Its sheltered location has been used as a haven for at least 350 years, but the present extensive breakwaters date from the late 19th century. The local community is augmented in spring and summer by hundreds of visitors from the large and popular residential caravan parks nearby. Maidens Bay is a sweep of 1.5 km of firm sand, with one notable exception. *Care must be taken to avoid a small patch of quicksands at a point near the Public Conveniences, where there are some not-very-well sited notices advising the public of this danger.* The area involved is small and not very obvious even when searching for it.

The Hogston Burn, whose shallow flow spreads out over the sand at the north end of the bay, is crossed by a small footbridge near a sign saying 'Welcome to Culzean Country Park', which marks the southern entrance and start of the Long Avenue leading through the policies of Culzean Castle and Country Park, which is owned by the National Trust for Scotland. This road, along which the Coastal Path now travels, is part of the original 18th century turnpike road marked on Captain Armstrong's 1775 map, which is shown crossing Maidens Bay and entering the long avenue past 'Cullean House', before dropping down on to the sands of Cullean Bay. (See map opposite)

At the start of the Long Avenue there stands a large sandstone slab into which is inserted an Honesty Box. Carved by the National Trust for Scotland's resident stonemason at Culzean, the surrounding inscription asks those entering the Trust policies to leave a donation towards the huge costs of up-keeping this wonderful property - held in trust for us all since 1945. *Please make a small contribution as a token of the great enjoyment and pleasure you are certainly about to experience as you traverse this beautiful estate. The National Trust for Scotland needs every penny you donate, and would appreciate it even more if you considered taking out Trust membership - which not only entitles you to free access to all NTS properties in Scotland, but also to all NT properties in England, Wales and Ireland as well. Great value for money!*

Armstrong's Long Avenue runs parallel to woodland and past an estate cottage to emerge near the Swan Pond with its lawns, cafe and toilet facilities. Here walkers have the choice of going round the west side of the Swan Pond to join a fine Cliff Walk sheltered by sycamore trees, which leads to Culzean Castle - or for those wishing to experience Culzean's magnificent woodland walks and gardens, there are alternative routes to the Castle and Country Park Visitor Centre from the Swan Pond. Either continue via the Long Avenue - and the superb Walled Garden - or take a right fork and enjoy a peaceful detour through the specimen trees of Happy Valley, before rejoining the Long Avenue north of the Walled Garden. On the right beyond the large car park, is the Deer Park with its fine resident herd of red deer, which is a great attraction for children and adults alike.

Walled Garden, Culzean

At the north end of the Long Avenue, just beyond the car park, the Coastal Path follows a road which dips down under a bridge-arch to emerge at the top of the path leading down to the Gas House and beach - and the Path's continuation along Croy Bay.

However, no walkers should be in such a big hurry that they would wish to leave Culzean Country Park and press on without paying a visit to the Castle and Visitor Centre. There are signs for both attractions at this point (*to which the walker should return to resume his northward journey*).

Designed for David, 10th Earl of Cassillis, by the famous architect Robert Adam, Culzean Castle was built from 1777 onwards, around the ancient tower house of yet another coastal Kennedy stronghold. When David died unmarried, the Earldom was inherited by Captain Archibald Kennedy a distinguished Royal Navy captain who, during the American War of Independence, unfortunately fell foul of both sides, lost half his estates, and had his New York town house - at No 1 Broadway - appropriated for the residence of George Washington. His son became the first Marquess of Ailsa.

The Castle and its 228 hectare grounds (563 acres) were handed over to the care of the National Trust for Scotland by the 5th Marquess of Ailsa in 1945; and shortly afterwards, the American wheel turned full circle when the people of Scotland, through the National Trust for Scotland, gave lifetime use of the top flat in Culzean Castle to General Dwight D Eisenhower - soon to become another American President - for his wartime efforts as Supreme Commander of the Allied Forces in the

Culzean Castle

liberation of Europe. Prominent in the castle is the Eisenhower Room, dedicated to a display of memorabilia of Ike's wartime experiences and his post-war visits to Culzean.

Culzean is the jewel in the crown of the NTS, who, in 1969, entered into an agreement with the Local Authority to manage the estate jointly as Scotland's first Country Park. The Visitor Centre - with the Rangers' Offices, information centre, shops and restaurant, all set within the attractive arched quadrangle of the old Culzean Home Farm (also designed by Robert Adam) - won major architectural awards when it was created in the 1970s.

Now Press on! Leave the Visitor Centre and walk back down the road that leads to the Castle. At the bottom of the brae, descend the 80 steps - or the 18th century road - to the old Gas House, which is situated by the shore in a small sheltered bay. This is also well worth a visit before strolling north along the sweep of Culzean - or Croy Bay as it is more popularly known. William Murdoch, the Scottish inventor of gas lighting, was born in Ayrshire, in the small village of Lugar, about twenty miles inland from Ayr.

If you have not already observed them from the castle ramparts, before moving on, in summer it can be worthwhile making a short detour south along the shore below the castle cliffs to see the fulmars which breed on the

Culzean and Ailsa Craig from road

cliffs and which can be recognised by their stiff straight-winged flight as they effortlessly glide the air currents. Set high in the cliffs are the entrances to several old smugglers' caves, which penetrate deep beneath the castle and originally may have had tunnels leading up into the castle itself. The Earls of Cassilis apparently did very well out of the smuggling trade - a prime case of 'one law for the rich . . !'

From the Gas House a path leads north beneath trees round the small bay, over a low rocky outcrop and past a holiday cottage on the beach. It continues along the shore under trees to the south end of Croy Bay, which is a mixture of sand, gravel, and small rocks at high tide, and thereafter continues on broad firm sand for 2 km. The cliffs rising from the beach are of lower old red sandstone - which is yellow!

At the north end of this popular picnic bay is Croyburnfoot Leisure Park, which as its name suggests, lies at the foot of the Croy Burn.

3.1m spring tide at Croyburnfoot - impassable for next 1.5 hours

Arran above Croy Bay

Interesting conglomerate rocks form the point at the Isle Port just north of the Caravan Park, and stretch back for about 100 m to the Croy Burn itself. Without a difficult rock clamber, this point might be impassable for an hour or two at the top of a high Spring Tide, when bare feet may be required to get round it - or even to ford the Croy Burn if it is running in spate over the beach. *During this time interval there is no public access through the Caravan Park, which is private property.*

From here, the walking is quite rough for the next 1 km, mainly over sand and heavy beach shingle, along to a track which ascends the escarpment in a series of hairpin bends from the foreshore - following the route of the 18th century shore road from Culzean to Ayr. *This area has been designated a Site of Special Scientific Interest (SSSI), on account of an ancient settlement by the shore just to the north of the track – with little to see but a few stones sticking up through the long grass.*

1.5 hours after same tide at Croyburnfoot. Now just passable at Isle Port.

At the top of the escarpment, a kissing gate leads to a double-fenced field-margin path that runs along the cliff-top to a steep gully and is forced inland to a small bridge over the Mill Burn. North of this bridge the Path again contours the cliff top past an old coastguard lookout post - from which a vigilant watch would have been kept on vital wartime Firth of Clyde shipping movements. The Path now arrives a sharp corner on the road running north from Dunure Mains Farm to the fishing village of Dunure. Beyond the bend, it traverses steeply down an old smugglers' path into Kennedy Park and the ancient ruins of Dunure Castle.

Dunure (population 492). The name Dunure apparently derives from the Gaelic *Dun-ure* - the 'Fort of the yew tree' - which would imply that there was an ancient fortification on the site long before the present Dunure Castle began as a cliff-top tower in the 14th Century. It was probably this earlier tower, which was attacked and captured by King Haco of Norway and his Vikings in 1263 on his way to eventual defeat at the Battle of Largs. Following this assault, the castle was progressively extended and strengthened as the power of the Kennedys grew, becoming their main stronghold and home of the Earls of Cassilis. During her tour of south-west Scotland and pilgrimage to Whithorn Priory, Mary Queen of Scots sojourned at Dunure from 4th to 7th August 1563, as guest of one of her staunchest supporters, Gilbert, 4th Earl of Cassilis; and one can imagine the sumptuous banquets and evenings of laughter and music conjured up for Her Majesty's entertainment by the good Earl.

Dunure Castle and Doocote

It was a very different form of entertainment seven years later in 1570, when Dunure Castle became famous for a notorious incident when Alan Stewart, the Commendator of Crossraguel Abbey in nearby Kirkoswald, was tied to a spit and twice roasted over a fire in the Black Vault by the selfsame Gilbert, in an attempt to extort the Abbey lands from him. The poor man was forced to sign over the lands, but later revoked his signature and complained to King James VI's Privy Council. The Earl's brutality received no more than a slap on the wrist by the Privy Council who compelled him to find security to leave the Commendator alone; and a few years later he was able to purchase the Abbey lands for a few thousand merks - while poor Alan Stewart never walked again due to the extent of his horrific burns. By such cruel means and worse, were many of our great estates acquired by their noble owners over the centuries.

Dunure and its 'creek' or inlet, must have been in existence as a fishing settlement, tucked in beneath and protected by its towering castle, long before it was first recorded in an official survey in 1655. By the end of that century, the castle had become ruinous, its great fortifications rendered useless by the advent of powerful cannons - and the end of the Carrick Feud. The Earls of Cassilis had moved their seat of power 10 kilometres inland to Cassilis Castle on the banks of the River Doon, and the 'useless' ramparts over the next two centuries served as a convenient quarry for stones to build the fishermen's cottages, the local limekiln, and the new harbour wall in 1811.

In the late 18th and early 19th century the harbour was used to smuggle tea, soap and whisky, but by 1847, this 'free trade' no longer flourished, and had been replaced by the honest endeavour of fishing - the harbour being home to a fleet of twenty boats. This fishing tradition continued till the 1950s, when fishing boats became too large for the small harbour and the fleet moved to Ayr. Many families with strong fishing connections still live in the village to the present day although inshore fleets have been decimated in the past twenty years, and any Dunure boats that are left now sail out of Troon!

Dunure Harbour

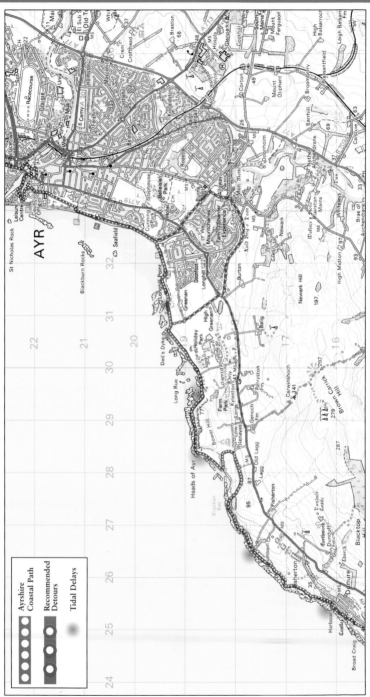

6. Kennedy Park - DUNURE Harbour – Beach track to Fisherton Bay – cliff top path and old railway track - Head of Ayr Caravan Park - Bracken Bay - Heads of Ayr Shore - Butlin's Bay – Deil's Dyke - Greenan Castle shore - Doonfoot Bridge – Blackburn Car Park - Wellington Square - St John's Tower - Cromwell's Fort - Loudoun Hall - Ayr Tourist Office, Sandgate - THE ANCIENT ROYAL BURGH OF AYR

Distance = 14.3 km = 8.9 miles

Car Parks: **Kennedy Park, Dunure - Doonfoot - Ayr Seafront**

Walking Summary: *Moderate/Difficult* – rocky escarpment/fields, livestock, rocky outcrops and shore, cliff top field path, railway track, sandy beach, promenade. Four short Tidal Stretches.

Points of Interest:	
Transport:	Good bus service
Historical:	Dunure Harbour - old port for sail-driven herring boats Dunure Castle - main Kennedy Clan coastal castle Birthplace of Robert Burns, Scotland's Poet - Alloway St John's Church Tower - seat of Bruce's first Parliament Cromwell's Fort Loudoun Hall - Ayr's oldest house Lady Cathcart's House - Birthplace of John Loudoun McAdam
General:	Dramatic views of Ailsa Craig, Ireland, Kintyre, Arran Ayr Harbour Ayr Beach - Popular in summer
Nature:	Roe Deer. Raptors. Finches and warblers. River Doon Estuary resident and migrating birds. Seals often seen, occasionally otters. Coastal geology. Raised beaches, agates, yellow sand stone and lava cliffs with smugglers' caves
Eating/Provisions:	Dunure - restaurant and pub Heads of Ayr Caravan Park Shop (summer) Doonfoot Store - 500m up river from Doonfoot bridge Seafield Store/Post Office - 100m east of dinghy ramp. Town Centre shops, pubs, and restaurants Ayr Seafront
Public Toilets:	Dunure Castle - Kennedy Park Blackburn Car Park on esplanade Near to childrens' play park at north end of Low Green North side of the New Bridge in River Street Arthur Street along Boswell Park from Sandgate
Accommodation:	Dunure and Farm B&Bs Camping at Heads of Ayr Caravan Park Visit Ayr Tourist Office for information Town Hotels and B&B s Camping - Craigie Caravan Park - north side of River Ayr (Check www.ayrshirecoastalpath.org)

High Level Optional Detour: Fit, more energetic walkers may wish to take a high level local path - involving a **5 km** detour over the top of the Brown Carrick Hill - to savour magnificent panoramic views of the Firth of Clyde and the Ayrshire hinterland.

Leaving the harbour, follow the roadside pavement north uphill to the Fisherton railway bridge. This cast iron bridge is a bit of a historical curiosity in itself. In its centre, on the platform side, is a strange large gap, now secured with section of wire mesh. One's first thoughts might be of a car accident or old age destroying the bridge panel, but closer examination reveals old brass hinges still attached to wooden battens on either side. This was no accident - but a gate in a most unusual place. As well as precious cargoes of early potatoes, the freight wagons often carried another precious cargo - pedigree Clydesdale brood mares brought from all over the country to Dunure to be sired by the Baron of Buchlyvie, the most famous Clydesdale breeding stallion of all time. From 1903 for ten years a procession of fine mares clip-clopped along the platform to be led up a steep and precarious ramp through the bridge gate and along the road to Dunure Mains.

Partly owned by William Dunlop of Dunure Mains, the Baron was for six years the subject of a famous and bitterly contested ownership court case, which went all the way to the House of Lords. The upshot was a bidding contest at Ayr market in 1911 between the two part owners in which Dunlop bought the stallion outright for £9,500 (£350,000 today!) Unfortunately for Dunlop, in 1914 the Baron's foreleg was broken by a kick from a mare and he had to be put down. But such was his fame that his skeleton was preserved and can still be seen in the newly refurbished Kelvingrove Museum in Glasgow.

Dunure Harbour

One hundred metres beyond the Fisherton railway bridge, on the far side of the A719, this high route follows the *Dunure to Maybole Footpath* up past Dunduff Farm and Dunduff Castle before branching off to the left along the side of a hilltop plantation and on to the ridge past the trig point to the wireless masts on Brown Carrick Hill. From here another path leads downhill on to a farm track which rejoins the A719 almost opposite the entrance road to Heads of Ayr Caravan Park, from where walkers will rejoin the main Path leading down to the shoreline at Bracken Bay.

Tide Warnings:
North and South of Dunure there are several points where at the top of a high spring tide the sea laps the bottom of rocky out-crops and cliffs to a depth of 0.1 - 1 metre. Spring tides occur twice a month over a period of several days – when the time of High Water is usually somewhere between 1100 and 1500 hours. If the tide is too big, the Coastal Path may be impassable for 1-2 hours either side of high water. By sensible planning, walkers can avoid unnecessary delays.

They should check Appendix I in the Guide Book in conjunction with the 'Admiralty EasyTide Tables' http://easytide.ukho.gov.uk, which give the times of High Water and also the Tidal Height for the day - and adjust their departure and arrival times accordingly. Packing a pair of plimsolls might be useful!

Links to this website can also be made through the Ayrshire Coastal Path Official Website (www.ayrshirecoastalpath.org.uk).

Having said all this, during the main walking months from April till October - there is no problem with walking along beach sections of the Coastal Path at any time of day for 25 days out of each month. Careful planning is all that is required.

Arran from Brown Carrick Hill

Normal Walking: After visiting the castle, follow the path down into the village and sample the atmosphere of its old fishing harbour and inn. The shingle beaches to the south and north of the harbour are noted for their agates, and are often frequented by beachcombers hunting for these elusive pebbles.

Walk round the harbour and along the sandy beach below the high sea wall of Dunure House, heading for the conspicuous cleft in the lava sill out-crop which forms a natural barrier at its north end. Beyond the cleft is a kissing gate, from which the path winds from beach to the escarpment and back to beach, avoiding gullies and rock outcrops that make walking difficult in places. Here the route is marked with white painted rocks and stone cairns, since marker posts would be quickly neutralised by heavy beef cattle looking for a scratching post.

During the summer months there are usually cows with suckling calves in this field, and walkers are advised not to take dogs along this stretch of Path because of the potential risk of an attack from cows trying to protect their calves. At times there may also be a beef bull in the field. While these are usually fairly docile when with a herd of heifers, it is the walker's responsibility to check for the presence of bulls or calves and to take appropriate action to give them a wide berth where possible, or seek an alternative route.

After 0.6 km, the Path leads to a lift-up stile through a stone march dyke, the top rail of which should always be lowered after crossing. From here the path again meanders for 300 m before dropping down a marshy gully on to Drumbain Beach and the first of the possible high tide hold-ups. At its north end is a rough scramble for 150 m over slippery rocks below a small waterfall and round the point into secluded Fisherton Bay.

N.B. *NO alternative route.* The private path which runs up the glen leads directly into Drumbain House garden; and the steep ground on the north side of the glen also leads into a private cottage garden. *Just plan to pass this point with plenty of time and tide to spare!*

Fisherton Gully Steps

The going is pleasant over shingle and sand to the north end of Fisherton Bay where a narrow stepped path - built from scratch by a squad of retired members of Ayr Rotary Club (you are only as old as you feel!) - traverses the base of a rocky outcrop, following a traditional roe deer track up the escarpment. Look out for footprints – if not deer. The stepped path winds up through a fairly steep gully, at the top of which is a kissing gate and the start of a short but spectacular field-edge cliff-top path offering great views of Arran on a good day – and some shelter behind a hawthorn hedge if it is raining! The bird life here is interesting, with ravens on the cliffs and eiders and shelduck on the sea below. If lucky, a hunting peregrine may be seen stooping at passing pigeons or waders.

[While it is possible at low tide to scramble along the remaining 1 km of foreshore to Bracken Bay, part of the going is very rough and dangerously slippery in places, and should only be attempted by fit and agile walkers. In addition there are several points where the sea covers the bottom of rocky out-crops and cliffs to a depth of 0.5 - 1 metre at any high tide and the route is normally impassable for 2-3 hours either side of high water. Not recommended.]

At the end of the second field, the Path curves uphill to join a section of the old Ayr to Turnberry line. The deep cutting which ran for 500 metres through this field has disappeared, having been in-filled many years ago; but enough remains to instil a sense of wonder at the huge investment of money and labour squandered in the building this railway a hundred years ago. The solum of the old railway track as it curves gently for 1 km round to Heads of Ayr Caravan Park provides fine firm walking and some of the best sea vistas of the entire Coastal Path - over Bracken Bay to the Heads of Ayr, across the Firth of Clyde to Arran and Loch Fyne, and northwards along the broad sweep of Ayr Bay to Ayr, Troon, Irvine and Ardrossan, beyond which on a clear day the distant peak of Ben Lomond may be seen rising proud of the Lochwinnoch Gap.

Gorse in bloom Bracken Bay

In Spring, the hillside is a yellow mass of flaming gorse, and the scrub is alive with the song of blackbird and thrush, linnet, chaffinch, goldfinch, and yellowhammer. Willow and sedge warbler, whitethroat and even grasshopper warbler can also be heard. In Autumn, the mass of hawthorn berries attract great numbers of fieldfares and redwings, while flocks of curlew and oystercatchers feed in the arable fields below while waiting for the ebb tide.

At the end of the line, just before reaching the Caravan Park, the Path slopes downwards through two kissing gates and becomes a field-edge path running for 200 m along the bottom of the embankment beneath a row of caravans to another kissing gate beside old bridge abutments leading through to Heads of Ayr Caravan Park.

From the old bridge abutments, the Path follows a public access farm-track, which runs seawards from Heads of Ayr Caravan Park alongside a field fence to a small triangular fir plantation on the escarpment overlooking Bracken Bay. Go through the kissing gate at the top of this brae and descend the old wrack road, which has been completely restored by Ayr Rotary Club, to the waterfall at the south end of Bracken Bay. N.B. At the top of the brae there are several gates with barbed wire wrapped round their top rails to deter people from climbing over them. Coastal Path walkers are asked not to use the grassy farm track leading from these gates down to an arable field at the north end of Bracken Bay. Casual walkers can sometimes be seen taking a short cut across this field to the beach, often damaging crops in the process.

The bluffs to the south of Bracken Bay are of old soft yellow sandstone and have been wind-carved into striking shapes by winter storms. Heading north along the bay on firm sand, the route continues under the

Bracken Bay

towering cliffs of the Heads of Ayr on a mixture of flat slabs of calciferous sandstone below the HW line, and on sand and small shore rocks above it. In contrast to the sandstone cliffs of the south end, the Heads cliffs are of soft, crumbling, unstable lava rock – and subject to rock-falls. *Because of the soft, unstable nature of both sets of rocks north and south of the bay, they should on no account be climbed.* In January 2008, a sudden rock-fall from the west cliffs of the Heads, crashed about 30 tonnes of lava rock on to the beach just at the point.

As in several other locations between Ayr and Girvan, *a small passage problem may present itself* for an hour either side of very high Spring tides. However, if northbound walkers can pass dry shod round the most westerly point of the Heads of Ayr, they should also be able to negotiate safely the next point one kilometre eastwards at Butlins Bay, where the high-tide line closes against a low crumbling bank for about 100 metres. Along this strip, a narrow, overgrown, rough path hugs the base of the slope and may help walkers avoid the boulder-strewn shoreline. At low tide, walking is much easier over the extensive flat slabs of sedimentary rock that form the shallow bed of what is still known locally as Butlin's Bay. Inland of the broad bay lies Craig Tara Holiday Park; a complex of static caravans on the site of what was once the famous Butlin's Holiday Camp.

Established by Billy Butlin in the 1930s, the camp was requisitioned by the navy during World War II and in 1942 became HMS Scotia - an important wartime Royal Naval Training Establishment.

After the War, the site was reclaimed by Billy Butlin, and from 1947 onwards, hundreds of thousands flocked there by special train (till the branch line finally closed in 1968), and by bus and car, for day trips or

3.0m High Spring Tide at east end of Heads of Ayr

3.0m tide - Just passable at east end of Heads of Ayr

annual holidays. Popular, much loved, and occasionally notorious, Butlin's Ayr Camp succumbed eventually to the continental package holiday phenomenon, but survived for a while as Butlin's Wonderwest Theme Park before being finally sold and converted into Craig Tara Holiday Park in the 1990s.

The bay curves along a kilometre of sandy beach to a volcanic sill called the Deil's Dyke, which juts out to sea and, like the Heads of Ayr, is difficult to negotiate at High Water Springs. However, at this point an easy alternative route leads up some wooden steps, across a field for 50 metres, and through a natural gap in the rock to drop down into a raised-beach meadow. From here, the walker return shore-wards to a small picturesque sandy bay dominated by the impressive, photogenic cliff-top ruin of Greenan Castle - a Kennedy tower house dating from around 1603.

Below the castle cliff there may be another small passage problem for one and a half hours either side of a very High Spring Tide. In which case, this can easily be overcome by following a track running up through the field past a cottage to a farm road that is part of the NCN7 cycleway. Followed north, it runs behind the castle, then downhill to pass along the foreshore to Doonfoot where it rejoins the Coastal Path.

If followed east to the A719, the NCN7 links with another new cycle track and bridle path, which leads to the Robert Burns Birthplace Museum. (see 6A -Detour to Robert Burns Birthplace Museum).

N.B. From Doonfoot, the Ayrshire Coastal Path and NCN7 share much of the same route through the towns of Ayr, Prestwick, Troon, and Irvine. In these urban areas walkers should follow the NCN7 blue signs - with the ACP Logo superimposed on every 3rd or 4th sign. However, walkers should keep on the lookout for small variations in the walking route - where the ACP signs will appear separately.

The joint route crosses a new footbridge over the River Doon and continues along the Promenade for 2 km towards Ayr Harbour. At the south end of Blackburn Car Park is the start of a *'Lang Scots Mile'* walk. Somewhat longer than the modern 1760-yard mile, its full 1984 yards (1814 m) to the swimming pool has been measured out in an attempt to encourage the good citizens of Ayr to improve their aerobic and cardiovascular fitness. Over to the right, lies the extensive common ground of the Low Green. Gifted to the town of Ayr in 1205 by William the Lion - at the same time as its Royal Burgh Charter - the integrity of *their* Low Green is still jealously preserved by Ayr townsfolk as an open space on which special events are held.

Here the Coastal Path diverges temporarily from the NCN7 and uses the meandering red path which runs across the Low Green to Wellington Square. This is a fine Georgian square laid out from 1814 onwards, which is bordered on its seaward side by the imposing classical columns of the County Court buildings, completed in 1822. by the north end of the path is an Ayrshire Coastal Path Information Board incorporating a plaque unveiled at the Opening of the Path on 28th June 2008. Thirty metres west of the Information Board is an interesting large commemorative stone plinth telling the history of the Low Green and William the Lion. The old county jail, which was attached to the western end of the Sheriff Court, was demolished after the First World War and replaced by another fine building, which became the administrative headquarters of Ayr County Council.

Ayr Low Green and County Buildings

Walk past the Sheriff Court entrance – which can be 'interesting' during sittings - and along Cassilis Street and Bruce Crescent to inspect a prominent tower flying the St Andrew's Flag. This is all that remains of St John's Church, where King Robert the Bruce held the first Scottish Parliament after the Battle of Bannockburn; and where Mary Queen of Scots supped and slept overnight on the first of August 1563 during her royal progress to Whithorn. It is well worth a visit to see the plaque commemorating Bruce's Parliament in 1315 - and also dozens of musket-ball pock marks made by Cromwell's troops using its lower walls for target practice during the time of the Commonwealth after the execution of King Charles I, Queen Mary's grandson.

St John's Church Tower

Cromwell's Fort

Cromwell's Citadel, which was constructed as a garrison fort in the years between 1652-1654, encompassed an area of 12 acres. Surrounded by a hexagonal rampart of earthworks faced with stonework, and cut off from the town by a moat dug between the river and the sea, it was built around St John's Church, the parish church, whose tower, was required as landmark for ships, and a military observation post. As a result, the townsfolk were deprived of their place of worship till Cromwell authorised the building of the Auld Kirk on the banks of the River Ayr in 1654.

Continuing along Montgomerie Terrace, the Path rejoins the NCN7 and follows the line of the old bastions and walls past Ayr Baths to the harbour side -where a recent modern housing development has replaced seven centuries of bustling piers and fish-market. It then leads past Loudoun Hall, an early 15th Century town house and former home of the hereditary Sheriffs of Ayr, which is Ayr's oldest remaining building. From here turn right up the Sandgate past the Town Hall (1826) with its magnificent spire, and adjacent fine Georgian buildings to the Ayr Tourist Office.

The Tourist Office is situated on the right-hand side of the Sandgate, in Lady Cathcart's House - a restored 16th Century town house - which is said to be the birthplace of yet another famous Ayrshireman - John Loudoun McAdam the Road Builder (1756-1836). Here walkers should be able to pick up a small map of Ayr Town Centre detailing other historic places of interest - such as the Kirk Port, the Auld Kirk and kirkyaird, and the Auld Brig o Ayr made famous by Burns's poem *'The Twa Brigs'* – which can be visited in a short historical detour before crossing the Auld Brig to rejoin the northward Coastal Path/NCN7 in Main Street.

> *Auld Ayr, whom ne'er a town surpasses*
> *For honest men and bonie lasses.*
>
> *Robert Burns*

Auld Ayr from New Bridge

The Ancient Royal Burgh of Ayr (population 46431) is a very attractive and bustling large town. Surrounded by beautiful rolling countryside, it has been endowed with a rich heritage of historic buildings, fine parklands and golf courses, excellent shopping and all amenities. Walkers should plan to stay for a few days, since there are many fine walks in and around the town, and lots to explore.

As the county town of Ayrshire, Ayr has an ancient history. Strategically situated at the mouth of the River Ayr, the county's largest river, it has been a place of settlement since Roman times. The origin of the name Ayr is uncertain. An early spelling was Air. An old word *Ar* means river, so the River Ayr possibly just means the River *'River'*. The wide river mouth became the focus for small trading ships, and in 1205 Ayr was created one of Scotland's earliest Royal Burghs by William the Lion, who built a royal castle on a mound on the south side of the river overlooking the harbour. Ayr was then primarily a garrison town protecting the south-western boundaries of his kingdom against the troublesome Lords of Galloway - the frontier being the River Doon. No trace of the castle now remains but its location is thought to have been the site now occupied by Ayr Academy.

Vikings found the long sandy strand of Ayr Bay perfect for their longship raids, and in 1263, King Haco of Norway landed here with his battle fleet and laid siege to the Castle of Ayr. The castle was well fortified and defended however, and presumably with greater concerns on his mind - like saving his strength to punish Alexander III King of Scots for evicting his ruling jarls from the Western isles - Haco abandoned the attempt and moved on up the Ayrshire coast to his eventual defeat at the Battle of Largs.

Galloway had become an integral part of the newly unified Scotland by this time, and its northwest district - *Carrick*, stretching from Glenapp to the River Doon - became the southernmost bailerie of the new Sheriffdom or Shire of Ayr. The other three were *King's Kyle* between the Rivers Doon and Ayr, *Stewart's Kyle* between the Rivers Ayr and Irvine, and *Cunninghame* from Irvine to the boundary with the Shire of Renfrew. Over time, the unique natural topography of each bailerie came to govern its agricultural specialisation. As the ancient rhyme put it :

> *Kyle for a man,*
> *Carrick for a coo,*
> *Cunninghame for butter an cheese,*
> *An Gallowa for 'oo.*   *'oo = wool*

After the internal battles fought to consolidate the Kingdom of Scotland, came the Wars of Independence to preserve it. Sir William Wallace features prominently in the history of Ayr and Ayrshire - with his frequent skirmishes against its English occupiers, and the slaughter of the town's garrison when he and his men burned down the Barns of Ayr. Both Wallace's parents were from old Ayrshire families, the Wallaces and Craufords, and Renfrewshire's claim on his birthplace at Elderslie is hotly disputed - with a strong Ayrshire counterclaim that he was in fact born at *Ellerslie* near Riccarton, Kilmarnock, since his father Malcolm Wallace had been born at the family seat at Riccarton; and his maternal uncle Sir Reginald Crauford was the Sheriff of Ayr.

Following his betrayal, capture by the English, and trial in Westminster Great Hall, Sir William Wallace was executed in 1305; but waiting in the wings was another son of Ayrshire, Robert Bruce, Earl of Carrick and a claimant to the Scottish throne. For the previous five years Bruce had been playing a dangerous game of political survival - alternately swearing fealty to Edward I of England in order to hold on to his large estates in the Borders, while at times supporting Wallace in forays against English garrisons.

Early in 1306, he made his move and was crowned King of Scotland at Scone - only to be driven thereafter into exile with a few followers on Rathlin Island off the Antrim coast where - as everybody knows - he consulted with a spider then moved back to Arran from whence, with

Traditional cargos of timber and coal - Ayr Harbour

three hundred followers, he made a D-Day landing at Turnberry in 1307. With this band of warriors he skirmished and fought in the Galloway and South Ayrshire hills for several years before his resounding triumph over the great army of Edward II at the Battle of Bannockburn in 1314.

Post Bannockburn, in 1315, the first meeting of Bruce's Scottish Parliament was held in the Church of St John the Baptist in Ayr. Here also, 250 years later, John Knox preached during the Reformation.

Over the next few centuries, as a county town with royal associations, which was visited on several occasions by James IV and Mary Queen of Scots, Ayr developed as an important trading port, and was thus described in 1578 - '*a prettie sey porte quhair strange natiouns oft arrives and their landes, the porte is sa commodious*'. About every hundred years however, the port was described as being in a ruinous state and, as the town depended on its maritime trade, large sums of money had to be spent on improvements. Oliver Cromwell recognised its importance in 1651 when he invaded Scotland and built the massive Citadel fort to command the Clyde and pacify the south west of the country. (See story of Ardrossan Castle chapter 9)

In 1732, Ayr entered the American tobacco trade as a nominated port - with a direct sailing to Chesapeake Bay - and on 6 June, the *Rebecca* of Ayr (a 100-ton brigantine) arrived with tobacco from Maryland. Twenty years later there were twelve Ayr ships on the American tobacco run; and from Ayr, tobacco was then often re-exported to France, Norway and the Baltic. Claret came from Bordeaux to Whigham's of Ayr - whose original cellars under Academy Street are still stocked with fine wine - and lime was imported from Ireland. Salted fish, mainly herring and cod, were also important exports.

Around 1772 when the first breakwaters were built, the piers on either side of the river could hold up to eighty ships - an amazing number. This was when the next major export industry began - one which continues to this day - the export of coal, with 12,900 tons of coal shipped in 1790. Much of this coal was hewn from coal pits north and south of the river mouth, whose workings extended under the sea.

During this period - the time of Robert Burns - Ayr had about 4000 inhabitants, and under the influence of the Agricultural and Industrial Revolutions it began to expand as a market and manufacturing town, as well as a seaport. By 1840, 50,000 tons of coal were being exported, by 1900 it was 500,000 tons, and by 1950 almost a million tons. In the years following the battle of Waterloo, fine Georgian and Regency houses were built to a regular plan south of the old medieval town, spreading out from Wellington Square and mimicking the concept of Edinburgh's New Town.

In 1840, the railway arrived in Ayr from Glasgow, and transformed the town's fortunes. As well as easy transportation of goods by freight train, passenger services now brought the first holidaymakers and day-trippers - escaping from the grime of Glasgow for a spell at the coast. This tourist boom made Ayr one of Scotland's premier holiday resorts for over a century - until the onset of cheap continental holidays in the 1960s. It still remains a very popular town for short breaks and day trips, with the added attractions of racing and golf - and Robert Burns.

Attracted by its pleasant environment, healthy mild climate, and ease of communication with Glasgow, many of the West of Scotland's great Victorian industrial magnates brought their wealth to Ayr and built their stylish mansions along Racecourse Road and the area round the old racecourse. These included Sir William Arrol, builder of the Forth Bridge, James Baird, ironmaster, and George Coats, thread manufacturer.

Many of Ayr's old industries - carpets, shipbuilding, heavy engineering, coal mining and fishing - are now gone; but the harbour, though it finally lost its traditional 700 year old fish market to Troon a few years ago, still exports coal and scrap iron, and imports timber, silica for glassmaking, and fertiliser. The paddle steamer *Waverley* calls regularly during the summer season and departs on day trips from Ayr harbour - an ideal opportunity for lingering walkers to experience a trip round Ailsa Craig, or see the Ayrshire Coastal Path from another perspective while sailing up the Clyde. For more intrepid walkers with a spirit of adventure, there is the option of stowing away on one of the huge luxury cruise liners which, several times a year, can be seen anchored in Ayr Bay while their passengers are ferried ashore to visit the Burns Country and Culzean Castle - or Edinburgh!

The old industries have largely been replaced by electronics and specialised engineering factories such those in the aerospace park at Prestwick Airport; by many small enterprising local industries; by service industries; by a very large expanding retail sector; and by employment in the local authority and health services.

Arran Sunset with Tree

6A. Branch Detour to ROBERT BURNS BIRTHPLACE MUSEUM (Local Path): Deil's Dyke - Greenan Cott – NCN7 east to A719 – Cycle way to ROBERT BURNS BIRTHPLACE MUSEUM - Doonfoot

Added Distance = **3.8 km = 2.4 miles**

Points of Interest:	
Historical:	Robert Burns's Cottage - Birthplace of Scotland's National Poet and composer of *Auld Lang Syne* Robert Burns Birthplace Museum (NTS - due to open 2009-10) Alloway Auld Kirk - features in *Tam o Shanter* Auld Brig o Doon -15th Century bridge - features in *Tam o Shanter*
General:	Village of Alloway Heads of Ayr Farm Park
Nature:	Interesting birdlife on river. Salmon leaping upstream - late summer and autumn. Otters - if lucky - and quiet!
Public toilets:	Robert Burns Birthplace Museum
Eating/Provisions:	Post Office and Chemist opposite Burns's Cottage Restaurant in village and at Robert Burns Birthplace Museum
Accommodation:	(Check www.ayrshirecoastalpath.org)

Burns Cottage

Alloway's Auld Hauntit Kirk

Walking: From the small bay south of Greenan Castle, walk up the field track past the cottage to join the National Cycleway NCN7 track which heads east inland for 800m to meet the A719 Dunure road. Cross this busy road carefully and follow a pleasant section of the old Ayr to Turnberry railway line, recently re-vamped as a local cycleway and bridle track, which runs east for 1.5 km till it crosses a bridge high above the River Doon - a well known salmon river - then passes through a short tunnel to arrive right in the middle of Alloway at the new Robert Burns Birthplace Museum being created by the National Trust For Scotland, which will replace the Burns Heritage Centre in 2009-2010.

In 2003, the National Trust of Scotland was invited to take over the Burns Heritage Park, which had previously been run by a triumvirate comprising the Burns Monument Trustees, South Ayrshire Council, and Scottish Enterprise Ayrshire. After several years of planning and fund-raising by the NTS, boosted by £5.5M from the Scottish Government, and £5M from the National Lottery Fund, at long last a Museum truly worthy of Scotland's most famous son is about to emerge from the soil of Alloway.

Very attractive, low profile, and eco-friendly, with an undulating sedum-roof, the new museum will house the priceless collection of Burns manuscripts, books, and other artefacts, in a state-of-the-art modern building which will protect them for all time from the ravages of dampness and leaking roofs to which they had been subject in the present antiquated building next to the cottage. The complex also incorporates superb educational, retail, and restaurant facilities.

A short 300-metre stroll south From the Birthplace Museum, will take the walker – like Burns's *Tam o Shanter* - past Alloway's Auld Haunted Kirk to the Auld Brig o Doon and the Burns Monument Gardens; and only 500 metres to the north of the Museum lies the world-famous Cottage - birthplace in 1759 of Robert Burns, Scotland's National Bard - which is a 'must visit' for any tourist to Ayrshire.

From the Cottage, walkers can choose either a direct route along busy Monument Road for 3 km (2 miles) into the centre of Ayr, or return seaward by walking 1.5 km down Greenfield Avenue to Doonfoot Store and along a pleasant riverside path to the mouth of the Doon to rejoin the Coastal Path/NCN7 which runs along the Promenade towards the harbour and town centre.

Auld Brig o Doon

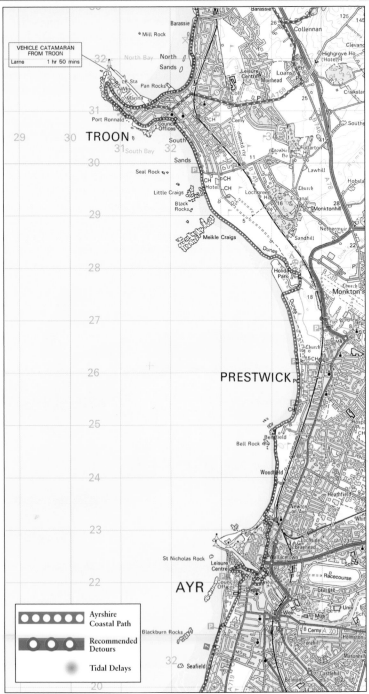

VEHICLE CATAMARAN
FROM TROON

Larne   1 hr 50 mins

TROON

PRESTWICK

Monkton

AYR

	Ayrshire Coastal Path
	Recommended Detours
	Tidal Delays

Thurs 3/3/11

7. AYR Tourist Office - High Street - Auld Brig o Ayr - River Street - Main Street – Peebles St - Limekiln Road - Newton Shore - Bentfield - PRESTWICK Promenade and Beach - Dune path by Old Prestwick Golf Course to bridge across Pow Burn - path past Prestwick Holiday Park and Royal Troon Golf Course to Troon South Sands - Troon Esplanade to TROON Harbour and Ferry Terminal.

Distance = 12.5 km = 7.8 miles

Car Parks: **Ayr Seafront – Troon Harbour Road**

Walking summary: *Easy* - promenade, pavements, paths, sandy beaches.

Points of Interest:	
Transport:	Trains from Glasgow and Stranraer
	Good bus service
	International and internal flights from Prestwick Airport
Historical:	Lady Cathcart's House - Birthplace of John Loudoun McAdam
	Loudoun Hall - Ayr's oldest house (early 16th Century)
	Ayr High Street
	Ayr Auld Kirk - built 1652
	Auld Brig o Ayr - 15th Century - immortalised by Robert Burns
	18th Century buildings south end of New Brig
	Bruce's Well - Maryborough Road
	Saltpans buildings - 18th Century
	Ballast Bank – Troon
General:	Ayr Harbour
	Prestwick Promenade and views across Firth of Clyde
	Old Prestwick Golf Course - first ever Open Golf Championship
	Royal Troon - Open Championship Golf Course
	Prestwick International Airport
	Wind and kite surfing off Troon South Sands
	Troon Harbour, Fish market, Yacht Haven
	RNLI Station and Troon Lifeboat *Jim Moffat*
	Ferry Terminal for Ireland
	Train Stations for Glasgow - Ayr, Prestwick (town/airport), Troon
Natural:	Shore birdlife
	Sea coal on Prestwick beach
	Seals off Troon and in Troon Harbour
Eating/Provisions:	Ayr Town Centre shops, pubs, and restaurants
	New Road shops and cafes
	Prestwick Town Centre shops, pubs and restaurants
	Troon Town Centre shops, pubs, and restaurants

Public Toilets:	River Street at New Bridge
	North end of New Road
	Prestwick seafront
	Troon South Beach
	Troon Ferry Terminal
Accommodation:	Booking at Ayr Tourist Office, Sandgate
	Visit Scotland, Main Street, Prestwick
	Camping at Craigie Caravan Park
	Hotels and B&Bs in Prestwick and Troon
	Camping at Prestwick Holiday Park
	(Check www.ayrshirecoastalpath.org)

Walking: From the Ayr Tourist Office, walkers have the choice of either going straight down Sandgate past the Town Hall and across the New Brig to join the Coastal Path/NCN7 route along Main Street – **or preferably**-walking down Sandgate and turning left into Boat Vennel to view Loudoun Hall, Ayr's oldest house. Then retrace your steps and cross over into High Street. Opposite the Fish Cross statue is the Brig Port leading up to and over the Auld Brig o Ayr, immortalised by Robert Burns in his poem *The Brigs of Ayr* – when the Auld Brig prophesised he would outlast the New Brig, recently built by Robert Adam in 1788, which latterly became unsafe and was demolished in 1877.

Auld Brig o Ayr

'This monie a year I've stood the flood an tide;
An tho wi crazy eild I'm sair forfairn,   *eild = old age*
I'll be a brig when ye're a shapeless cairn!'

Continue up the same side of the High Street for a hundred metres to the Kirk Port, under whose arch is an old iron mortsafe, used in former times to enclose newly buried coffins until their inhabitants were well past their sell-by date and no longer marketable by unscrupulous early 19th Century body snatchers in their quest to supply bodies for anatomical dissection by equally unscrupulous, client Medical Anatomy Departments.

Beyond the Kirk Port arch lies the venerable Auld Kirk, the building of which was funded by Oliver Cromwell in 1654. Stroll through the interesting auld kirkyaird with its Covenanters' Graves and those of contemporaries of Robert Burns, and turn left down the river to cross and pause for a minute on the 15th Century Auld Brig, which itself was on the point of collapse before it was completely restored in 1907.

Now turn left again along River Street to the New Brig, and walk along Main Street past the Carnegie Library. Cross Main Street at the lights and continue on the Coastal Path/NCN7 route along Peebles Street, Waggon Road and Glebe Road to Limekiln Road, where over to the right is the Ayr Curlers' Ice Rink (Remember Ailsa Craig?). The NCN7 and Coastal Path route leads over the railway bridge at the Gasworks and round the corner down to Newton esplanade. *Take great care as this short 200m section of road carries heavy goods vehicles to Ayr Port, and there is no pavement for over 100 metres.*

With even a moderately strong onshore wind at high spring tides, waves will break over the seawall along the exposed Newton promenade. In gale force winds it is positively dangerous, and great care must be taken - and a wide detour made across the flat open green till past the danger. It may even be necessary for walkers to retrace their steps along Limekiln road to Tam's Brig and walk along the main Prestwick Road to Maryborough Road, which leads down to Prestwick promenade.

At the north end of the seawall, a rough track runs along the seaward edge of St Nicholas Golf Course, thereby avoiding a rough and rocky armoured stretch of shore, impassable at high tide. The golf course is private land, and any pedestrians walking on this path do so at their own risk with regard to flying golf balls. *They must also remember basic golfing etiquette - have the courtesy to stand still and quiet while someone is playing a shot – and keep a good lookout for golf balls.* Before Bentfield Point, the Coastal Path branches down a new ramp leading through the armoured rock embankment on to the beach, and detours round the sand and shingle shoreline beneath the houses on Bentfield Point.

Using this new shore route will avoid disturbance to golfers since the existing path continues along the top and crosses in front of several tees and greens on the course. It will also reduce the considerable risk of injury to any foolhardy walkers thinking of taking the top path, which heads straight into the flight line of golf balls being hit over a blind summit!

The Ancient Burgh of Prestwick (population 14934). It is just before Bentfield Point, that walkers leave Ayr and enter **Prestwick**, which was granted its charter sometime between 1165 and 1173, thus claiming to be an older burgh than its more illustrious and larger neighbour the Royal

Burgh of Ayr. The name means 'Priest's dwelling', and the roofless remains of 12th century St Nicholas Church, still standing on a knowe opposite the station and Old Prestwick golf course, can be clearly seen from the dune path bordering the course.

Once round Bentfield Point, a short 400 m detour up Maryborough Road leads to the site of an ancient Hospice for lepers - and Bruce's Well - once visited for its supposed curative powers by King Robert the Bruce, who was said to have been afflicted by a form of this disease.

Old 18th century Saltpan Buildings

Back on the shore, at the start of Prestwick Promenade, are two striking old twin buildings -18th Century Saltpan houses - used to dry salt from seawater, which was boiled using locally mined coal. The final product was used mainly to salt and preserve the huge tonnage of herring landed at Ayr harbour.

Prestwick Beach

The promenade now stretches for 2 km, passing a kiddies' playpark, which was once the outdoor unheated swimming pool for Prestwick's hardy citizens. After the coming of the railway, Prestwick, like Ayr, became a very popular seaside resort, but remained a much smaller town. For many years, its main sources of employment were the collieries whose workings ran for miles out under the sea. A thousand men were once employed at Glenburn Pit, which closed in 1973. As mentioned earlier, these jobs have been replaced with skilled labour at the complex of aerospace-related engineering works and other factories built on the old colliery site adjacent to Prestwick Airport.

From this point on the promenade, a 400 m detour along Links Road towards the Town Centre will take walkers past Old Prestwick Golf Clubhouse. *Prestwick Golf Club was founded in 1851; and it was on this famous links course that the first-ever Open Golf Championship was contested in 1860.* Twelve championships were held at Prestwick before any other links courses - such as St Andrews - were ever involved. This first Open Championship is commemorated with a small cairn at the roadside just before the clubhouse.

The Railway Station is situated a few metres beyond the clubhouse; and a further kilometre on - through Prestwick Cross and north along the A79 - is Glasgow Prestwick International Airport. Turning south at the Cross takes walkers along Main Street, the town's shopping centre.

Prestwick Airport has a long and distinguished history. It began as a local grass airstrip for small planes in 1934, and a year later, the ground was purchased by D F McIntyre and the Marquis of Clydesdale, *who in 1933 had been the first aviators to fly over Mount Everest.* Here they founded Scottish Aviation Ltd, an elementary flying training school with 16 Tiger Moths. With the outbreak of war in 1939, it became RAF Prestwick under the command of Group Captain D F McIntyre, and quickly became strategically the most important air terminal in the UK, since most of the aircraft used in the later stages of the War in Europe - some 20,000 in all - were ferried across the Atlantic via Newfoundland and Iceland to Prestwick, and onwards to bases in England and elsewhere. A US Air Force base was set up on the north side of the airport in 1942. In the single month of August 1944, just after D-Day, the incredible number of 7,847 aircraft movements was recorded.

Prestwick Airport's main advantages were in being close to the Gulf Stream, close to America, far from Germany, and enjoying good, fog-free, mild weather conditions. To the ferry pilots it became famously known as 'The Hole in the Clouds' due to its peculiar and welcome characteristic - surprised pilots suddenly relieved to find clear sunny weather over Ayr, Prestwick and Troon, when there was heavy cloud over the hills to the north, south and east, and over Arran and the Atlantic to the west. This is due to geography - a combination of the low lying basin in which these towns sit, surrounded by hills; and the fact that the mountains of Arran often seem to divert clouds and rain showers to the north and south of Ayr Bay.

One of Prestwick's most famous ferry pilots was Amy Johnston, who in 1930 had flown solo in a single-engined biplane from England to Australia. In January 1941, she left Prestwick to fly down to Oxford, stopping off at Blackpool to visit her sister. Ignoring advice not to fly on because of bad weather, she continued her trip, and crashed into the Thames Estuary. Her body was never found.

After the war, Prestwick became Scotland's international gateway to America, but by the mid 1960s it went into decline as British Airports Authority concentrated all its resources into developing Glasgow Airport - and starved Prestwick of investment. In the early 1990s however, the airport's fortunes changed dramatically when it was bought from BAA by a consortium that included the local District Council. A small Irish airline, Ryanair, was persuaded to fly a triangular route from Prestwick – London - Dublin. The rest is history! Ryanair is now one of the most powerful low cost airlines in Europe, and Prestwick one of its main bases. Passenger numbers have risen from 300,000 in its old Trans-Atlantic heyday, to 2,500,000 per year and rising, and it is now also the UK's second largest transatlantic freight cargo airport.

From 1971, the former US Air force base has been occupied by HMS Gannet. As Royal Naval Air Station Prestwick, HMS Gannet was home to nine antisubmarine warfare Sea King helicopters which protected the approaches to the Firth of Clyde and also flew Search and Rescue missions. Though all its ASW helicopters were transferred to Cornwall following defence cuts after the end of the Cold War, HMS Gannet has continued to perform a vital role since 2002 as *HMS Gannet SAR Flight* using two specially equipped Sea Kings.

Gannet has been consistently one of the busiest Search and Rescue units in the British Isles, covering as it does - within a radius of 300 miles - an area which includes the Lake District, Irish Sea, Northern Ireland, Hebrides, and the Southern Highlands as far north as Ben Nevis. Averaging 250 callouts per year over the past eight years, it is regularly the UK's busiest SAR station, and in 2007 shattered the UK record, responding to 359 'shouts' and rescuing 349 people from dangerous situations. On any day along the Coastal Path, walkers will

HMS Gannet SAR Sea King with Author on board.   *Photo: Helen Begg*

inevitably catch a glimpse of Gannet's distinctive red-nosed Sea King en route to 'a shout', or undertaking a training flight over the Clyde.

On returning to the beach play-park, the Coastal Path runs to the end of the promenade, from where the walker has a choice of route. It is a pleasant walk along the sands, and if the tide well out, the Pow Burn low, and the water warm, there is a barefoot paddle across the burn to reach Troon south beach. While walking along the shore, look out for patches of small black 'pebbles' stranded by the receding tide. On closer inspection these will be found not to be stone pebbles - but sea coal. The rock strata rise from west to east, and fragments of coal break off from the ends of coal seams exposed on the seabed.

If the tide is full, the burn in spate, the winds too strong or the water too cold, there are three further options. The first is to follow a well-trodden track from the estuary back alongside the golf course practice ground on the western bank of the tidal creek to a bridge over the Pow Burn.

The second, requiring a bit more forethought, is to cut in early from the shore about 600 m short of the Pow Burn through a gap in the dunes - marked by a large pole - and join the designated Coastal Path route which runs east for 400 m along the northern boundary of the golf course to the same bridge – thus saving a 1500 m detour.

A third option is to cut up before the circular pump station at the end of the promenade, and enjoy a walk along the dune-top path with its inland views over the golf course and the airport, to join the Coastal Path at the far end of the course. *This area is ecologically very fragile, and great efforts are continually being made to protect the four-kilometre line of sand dunes - which in turn protect both Prestwick and Royal Troon Championship courses - from severe wind erosion. Please keep off the dunes as much as possible, and preferably walk along the shoreline.*

Beyond the first road bridge go through a kissing gate, turn left and follow the Sewage Pump Station access road adjacent to Prestwick Holiday Park. From here the Path runs alongside and outside the boundary of the Holiday Park to the Prestwick Golf Club's boundary with Royal Troon, then runs parallel with the east bank of the Pow Burn skirting the southern end of Royal Troon Golf Course - also the famous home of many recent Open Championships - to emerge on to Troon South Sands by another large marker pole.

Troon Promenade

White posts on the crest of the dunes mark the out of bounds limits of the golf course. This is a windy beach, and as such is very popular with windsurfers and kite-surfers - so watch out for large rogue kites. Offshore lie the Meikle Craigs, (Scots for 'the big rocks') which extend out to sea for almost a kilometre and must form a potential hazard to careless sailors when covered at high tide.

Troon (population 14766). If they wish, walkers can leave the beach and join the esplanade at the north end of Royal Troon Golf Course. The eroded dunes bordering the esplanade have also been consolidated and markedly improved by the commendable efforts of the Troon Dune Restoration Project. These dunes, planted with sea buckthorn and rosa rugosa, will provide walkers with welcome shelter from strong winds and blowing sand as the Path continues along the esplanade in a broad sweep to the Ballast Bank. Halfway along, standing on the green sward near an opening that leads to the South Beach Hotel, is a small stone bollard whose faded inscription tells that it marks the 'Northern boundary of the Port of Ayr'. From the top of the Ballast Bank, there is a fine view beyond the timber sheds over the harbour and marina to the long curve of Irvine Bay. On a clear day, Ben Lomond can be seen through the Lochwinnoch Gap.

Troon, like Girvan, Ayr and Prestwick, also benefited from the railway and became a fashionable holiday resort and desirable place in which to live. Many wealthy people over the past hundred years have built their exclusive villas and mansions in the neighbourhood of Troon south beach - no doubt attracted by the fresh sea air, the proximity to Glasgow - not to mention the famous links golf courses.

The name Troon literally derives from *an t-sron* - Gaelic for 'the nose' - which exactly describes the long promontory on which the Ballast Bank is built, and which shelters Troon Harbour from the prevailing south westerly winds. Around 1608, this ancient sheltered anchorage was first developed as a harbour by the Burgh of Irvine. Two centuries later, in 1808, the north pier was built by the Duke of Portland - forming the biggest harbour in Ayrshire - to allow the export of coal from his Kilmarnock mines, nine miles inland. This coal was transported on horse-drawn waggons along the first commercial rail track in Scotland - *and across the world's first railway viaduct*. Very soon, Kilmarnock weavers and miners were coming down to Troon in the empty horse-drawn coal waggons for a Sunday at the seaside - the world's first rail travellers!

The Ballast Bank is basically a high, elongated mound formed from ballast dumped over the past two centuries by incoming sailing colliers before they were loaded. By 1846, 130,000 tons of coal were being exported annually from Troon. The Ballast Bank provides a fine panoramic view landward as well as seaward. The Southern Upland hills, from Black Craig in Glen Afton, westwards to the Rhinns of Kells and the Merrick Range, can be easily identified from this viewpoint as they rim the southern horizon and stand out in the clear visibility of a north westerly air-stream. At 843 metres or 2764 feet, the Merrick is the highest hill in the south of Scotland.

Ballast Bank, Troon

Troon is still a busy and expanding harbour, owned by Associated British Ports, which is now home to the former Ayr fishing fleet and fish market, and the RNLI Station and Troon lifeboat *Jim Moffat*. Timber cargoes are imported from Arran and the Kintyre peninsula by ship and barge to Troon's large sawmill and the Irvine pulp mill; and there are also freight ferry and daily car and passenger fast catamaran sailings to Northern Ireland. The yachts from Troon Marina and Troon Cruising Club in the inner harbour will sail the waters of the Clyde, or round the Mull of Kintyre into the magnificent cruising grounds of the Western Isles during the summer season - while each year some intrepid sailors will leave on extended voyages northwards to Shetland, Faeroes, Iceland, Norway and Sweden; or south to Ireland, the Scillies, Brittany, Portugal or the Mediterranean.

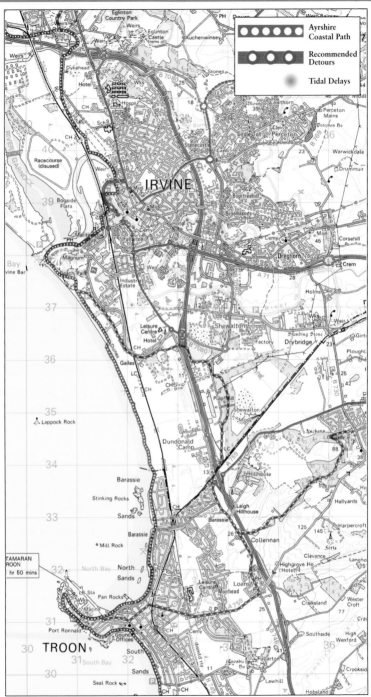

8. Short Beach Route - TROON Harbour - Barassie shore - Irvine Beach Park and Harbour - ANCIENT BURGH OF IRVINE (Also see 8A)

Distance = **10 km = 6 miles**

Car Parks: **Troon Harbour Road – Irvine Beach Park**

Walking summary: *Easy* - promenade, pavements, paths, sandy beaches.

Points of Interest:	
Transport:	Train service Good bus service Ferries to Northern Ireland
Historical:	Tide Telegraph Ship Inn and old Harbourside dwellings Eglinton Trophy, Cunninghame House (see **10A**) Seagate and Seagate Castle Glasgow Vennel
General:	Distant views of Southern Uplands Ayr and Irvine Bay seascapes Bridge of Scottish Invention Magnum Leisure Centre Scottish Maritime Museum Irvine town centre
Nature:	Sea and Shore birds - Troon North Sands Fragile dune and heathland ecology Estuary birds on Bogside mudflats
Eating/Provisions:	Templehill shops, pubs and restaurants Troon Morrisons Barassie shops and cafe Irvine shops, pubs and restaurants
Public Toilets:	Barassie shore Irvine Beach Park
Accommodation:	Troon B&Bs, Guesthouses and Hotels List of Accommodation Irvine Beach Park (Check www.ayrshirecoastalpath.org)

Walking: Walkers now have a choice of routes to Irvine - a 10 km (6 miles) stroll along the sands to Irvine - or a somewhat longer journey of 19 km (11.5 miles) to incorporate a visit to the ancient Royal Castle of Dundonald. Dundonald Castle is famous as the birthplace of the Stuart Dynasty of Kings and Queens of Scotland and later - from 1603 - of Great Britain.
(See Route 8a).

Troon Yacht Haven

Leave the Harbour and walk past the sawmill, Yacht Haven and Troon Cruising Club to the P&O Ferry Terminal roundabout. Just beyond this roundabout turn left on to the grassy bank and follow a pleasant shore path away from the traffic past the Pan Rocks to the car park. Rejoin the roadside pavement for a short distance before veering on to the long ribbon of cycle path leading to the far end of the North Green. In front of you, sweeps a great expanse of sandy beach stretching 13 km (8 miles) from Troon to Saltcoats, seemingly continuous, but bisected and impassable halfway along its length where the River Irvine bursts through the formidable barrier of sand dunes.

Though the going is excellent along firm sand all the way to Irvine, it can be tiring and occasionally boring, so walkers should embrace the variety of terrain offered by the cycle path and the broad grassy sward that extends the length of Barassie foreshore. In so doing, they may also reduce their risk of being garrotted by the guy wires of wayward, kite-driven land yachts, which regularly and spectacularly race along this section of beach whenever there is a good breeze and the tide is out. When the tide is in, the land yachts are replaced by wind surfers and acrobatic kite surfers - with both groups providing equally spectacular displays of speed and agility. There are official warning notices asking beach walkers to be aware of guy wires and to keep clear of the kite surfers. The tide goes out a long way over Troon North Sands, and during the autumn and winter months this inter-tidal area is an important feeding ground for migrant shore birds, and a great draw for bird watchers.

Barassie Bay north to Irvine

When walkers join the strand at the far end of Barassie, they are entering North Ayrshire. *In the interests of coastal conservation they should again walk along the sand rather than on the dunes. Dune systems are very fragile all along the coast from Prestwick to Saltcoats, and - like South Ayrshire Council and Troon - North Ayrshire Council and the Irvine Bay Urban Regeneration Company are trying to protect their dunes from further serious erosion, by marking access points through the dunes with tall posts topped with a black diamond.*

Hidden behind the dunes are several of Ayrshire's finest links golf courses, Barassie, Western Gailes, and Glasgow Gailes, beyond which looms the large complex of Irvine Pulp Mill. Finnish-owned, it specialises in making glossy paper for quality magazines, and is contracted to take much of the timber harvested from the spruce and pine forests of upland Ayrshire and Galloway.

If happy with sand underfoot and a light sea breeze on their cheeks, walkers can enjoy a pleasant stroll along 5 kilometres of beach right to the mouth of the River Irvine; but if a strong wind is blowing sand in their eyes or knocking them off their feet, they can escape from the fury of the elements through a gap in the dunes - *identified by a large marker post topped by a white band* - at the northern boundary of Western Gailes golf course, and enjoy the shelter of a well-trodden path, which runs behind and parallel to the high dunes and provide an excellent windbreak all the way to Irvine. It is interesting terrain, with marram grass coastal vegetation intermingled with acid heath-land broom, gorse, heather and dog roses. During the war, this area was occupied by the Royal Ordinance Factory Irvine, employing 2000 workers; and was later an army rifle range. Pity the poor burghers of Irvine - saddled with an ammunition dump on the south side of the town, and Britain's biggest explosives factory on the north!

Several pine shelterbelts break up the heath-land, and one section seems to be used as a quad bikers' track - which if it keeps noise and disturbance off the beaches and away from the walking public and wildlife, is a good thing. Beyond this track is a flat area on which are laid out some very large, strange, inter-connecting gravel circles. Although they look somewhat like alien-inspired crop circles, the ground is, in fact, a caravan site used occasionally for large rallies.

Just beyond here the Path enters Irvine Beach Park, which is a large area of reclaimed land adjacent to the massive Magnum swimming pool and ice rink leisure complex, attractively landscaped with paths and ponds.

At its southernmost extremity is a sandstone lookout shelter sculpted in the shape of a large stone dragon with fine views over the majestic sweep of Ayr and Irvine Bays - with far Ailsa Craig standing sentinel on the south west horizon, Arran looming ever closer in the west, and the Paps of Jura peeking over the distant Kintyre peninsula. As well as the occasional cruise liner visiting Ayr Bay, it is common to see one or two huge bulk carriers or container ships at anchor in Irvine Bay - especially in offshore winds - as they await clearance from the Clyde Port Authority to berth at Hunterston Deep Water Terminal, or the container port at Greenock.

Dragon Viewpoint, Beach Park, Irvine

A short distance out to sea lie two channel markers, which guide small vessels over the harbour bar and into the narrow river entrance. The square tower at the point was formerly used as a Tide Telegraph to tell ships wishing to enter Irvine harbour the depth of water over the bar at any state of the tide. As part of an ingenious system invented in 1904 by the local harbourmaster, floats in a large tank at the water's edge were connected by pulley and chain to the tower, and to black balls attached by rope and pulley to the rooftop frame. As the tide and the floats rose, so did the number of balls that could be seen above the roof; and as the tide fell, so did the number of balls visible. At night, the number of lights visible through shaded windows on the seaward wall would be the same as the number of balls seen by day. Although disused now for many years, the float tank is still in situ, and several black balls lie inside the fence.

Just upstream, is the 'Bridge of Scottish Invention', which carried visitors over to the Big Idea Inventor Centre till it closed its doors in September 2003. Fretted metal panels on the bridge detail the inventions of an impressive list of 24 famous Scots - Napier, Watt, Black, Murdoch, Telford, Simpson, McMillan, Maxwell, Symington, Kelvin, McAdam, Bain, Young, Thomson/Dunlop, Lister, Ramsay, Bell, Dewar, Baird, Wilson, Fleming, Watson-Watt, and Donald. How many do you know? . . . Have a guess!

Bridge of Scottish Invention

Those who are not aware of the worldwide influence of these Scotsmen on all our lives, will have to wait until they cross the bridge and read the legends, to discover and appreciate the depth and diversity of Scottish inventiveness and genius over the centuries. *(Meantime, it would be helpful if an Information Board could be placed at the south end of the bridge to impart this knowledge to walkers and other visitors now.)* Near the bridge is a Tourist Information Board containing a very useful list of local B&B, Guesthouse and Hotel accommodation.

The Irvine Bay Urban Regeneration Company (IBURC) has recently been constituted to revitalise the environment and industry of Irvine, Kilwinning, and The Three Touns – Stevenston, Saltcoats and Ardrossan. The Bridge of Scottish Invention is a key part of this project, but sadly walkers and others may have to wait for three to five years until the development plans for the Big Idea site are fully realised, and the bridge is finally re-opened to provide access to the short beach route between Irvine and Stevenston.

Until then, the Ayrshire Coastal Path and NCN7 cycleway combine once more - just beyond the Magnum Centre - to take the long historic route north, skirting round the impassable natural barriers formed by the tidal River Irvine and the dangerous mudflats and flood plain wetlands of the Garnock Estuary. As before, for the guidance and reassurance of walkers, the ACP logo is incorporated into a proportion - but not all - of the NCN7 signage.

This route has been used from time immemorial by travellers from Ayr to Glasgow or the Upper Clyde Coast, passing through Irvine and then the abbey town of Kilwinning, which prospered from its strategic position at the first crossing point of the Garnock Water and the fork of two major trade routes. Stevenston, Saltcoats and Ardrossan also benefited at a later period when coal exploitation began at the beginning of the Industrial Revolution.

Irvine Harbourside

The Ancient Royal Burgh of Irvine (population 33090):
In the distance beyond the Magnum Leisure Centre complex can be seen the spires and rooftops of the ancient seaport and **Royal Burgh of Irvine**, now a mile inland from the sea and half-hidden by the attractive vernacular new buildings of Harbourside, and the industrial estates to its south west.

Upstream of the Magnum, moored on Irvine harbour's redundant jetties, lie many vessels collected over time by the Scottish Maritime Museum, with a vast collection of heavy engineering exhibits housed in the Stephens of Linthouse Engineering Shed - which was dismantled, transported to Irvine, and re-erected, when that famous Clydeside shipyard closed in the nineteen sixties.

The Maritime Museum is well worth a visit - to infuse us all with justifiable pride in the Clyde and Scotland's incomparable maritime heritage. The old Harbourside area has been re-developed over recent years in a most sympathetic style, with new houses and buildings like the Harbour Arts Centre blending in very well with the Museum and several ancient inns and dwelling houses, including the old Ship Inn which was built in 1597 and restored in 1754.

Carter and Clydesdale

Irvine vies with Ayr for the title of the oldest town in Ayrshire, having received its Royal Charter about the same time, around 1200. Long before this, with its natural harbour, river crossing points and shelter provided by the dunes, it was an obvious place for human settlement. The origin of the name Irvine is unclear, but from old spellings like Irewin it may simple mean: 'The river with the wind or bend' (*Ar* = river and *winda* = bend), which aptly describes its tortuous course to the sea.

In medieval times, Irvine harbour was well inland from its present site, and was situated at the foot of the Seagate, near Seagate Castle. Irvine vigorously competed with Ayr for commerce, and was thus described by Bishop Leslie in 1578:

> *'the toune of Irvine, quilke in peple, in riches, and commodiousness of the Sey porte is nocht mekle inferiour to Air'.*

Until 1668 when Port Glasgow was founded, Irvine served as the seaport for Glasgow, with goods for export being transported on horseback the 26 miles from Glasgow. Though Greenock was 23 miles from Glasgow, Irvine's situation on the lower Clyde gave ships an easier passage in open sea. However, the old harbour silted up easily, and eventually in 1665, a start was made on a new harbour, which occupies the present site. Although this enterprise came too late to save losing their Glasgow trade to Port Glasgow, Irvine harbour continued to prosper - with coal exports of 24,000 tons to Dublin in 1793, using fifty-one vessels from 33 to 160 tons.

The main imports were hides and grain from Ireland, hemp and iron, and timber from Norway and Wales for shipbuilding. Traditional smuggling of grain from Ireland, and whisky from Arran, was overshadowed in the 1760s and 1770s by large scale smuggling of tea, West Indian rum, tobacco and brandy, organised by legitimate Irvine firms via Ireland and the Isle of Man.

Shipbuilding was an important industry for two centuries, and it is almost impossible to believe that ships as large as 10,000 tons were being built at the Ayrshire Dockyard in the run up to the 1914-18 War. Nowadays the skippers of 5-ton yachts worry about getting safely over the un-dredged harbour bar!

Fifty years ago, Irvine was a modest-sized small burgh with a population of 16,000, and with several major local industries in post-war decline. Like many other UK cities, Glasgow's Victorian slums were overcrowded, and a strategic planning decision was made by the British Government to establish New Towns throughout the country, in order to redistribute the population and relieve inner-city pressures. Irvine was designated a New Town with a projected population of 100,000, and Irvine Development Corporation was set up to plan and oversee its development.

A huge industrial estate was set up at Shewalton, to the south east of the town, to which were attracted many major firms such as Beechams, Monsanto and Hyster, among others. While the town's population has never reached its 100,000 target - due largely to the unforeseen influence of 'The Pill' - it has flourished and still continues to rival Ayr in size and influence.

Its rapid expansion, however, was not without great pain. Typical of the nationwide planning decisions which bedevilled the 1960s and left a

The Seagate and Seagate Castle, Irvine

lasting blight on most of our Scottish towns, the ruthless, insensitive demolition of many of Irvine's 18th century vernacular dwellings to make way for that monstrous box of shops which hangs over the River Irvine, has ripped much of the heart and character out of the historic burgh. Enough remains, however, to give visitors an idea of Irvine's ancient past, and a short detour through the Town Centre is to be recommended.

Follow the route signs and turn left at the top of Montgomerie Street, then go round the Victoria roundabout and under the Railway Bridge. Once past Fullarton Church, the NCN7 runs parallel the road and through an underpass to reach the waterside and a footbridge over the River Irvine. Once across the river and the Low Green, walkers arrive at the foot of Seagate - the ancient street that led up from the medieval harbour to the town. On this street still stands Seagate Castle, the town house of Hugh, Earl of Eglinton, who entertained Mary Queen of Scots and her Four Marys at nearby Eglinton Castle, when they stayed there overnight on 1 August 1563 while on a pilgrimage to Whithorn.

Turning right at the top of Seagate takes walkers past the Irvine Burns Club Museum to The Cross, the Briggate and High Street. Here, in mid-August, is held the Marymas Fair, whose horse racing traditions go back many centuries. The Carters' Society, which dates from 1670, still plays a major part in the grand procession through the town after the crowning of the Marymas Queen at the Mercat Cross - and later the carthorse and pony racing held at the Cadgers' Racecourse on the Town Moor.

In 1781, Robert Burns moved to Irvine from his father's farm to live at a house in Glasgow Vennel for two months, and learn the trade of flax dressing - an early example of a struggling Ayrshire farmer trying to diversify to make ends meet, and a struggle that continues to this day. Glasgow Vennel lies just off the High Street, and the thatched cottages in which Burns lodged and worked are now a museum.

Walkers should now retrace their steps to the footbridge.

Footbridge over River Irvine

8A. Longer Inland Detour via DUNDONALD and The Smugglers'
Trail – a new local walk – to IRVINE:-   (Also see Route 8)

i) TROON Harbour - Templehill - Portland Street - A759 - Loans –
Smugglers' Trail via Troon Reservoir - Dundonald Woods -
DUNDONALD CASTLE and Visitor Centre

Distance = 7.6 km = 4.1 miles

ii) DUNDONALD CASTLE – Smugglers' Trail - Troon Reservoir –
A759 to Dundonald roundabout - National Cycle Network (NCN7) -
Shewalton Woods - Gailes - Irvine Beach Park and Harbour -
ANCIENT BURGH OF IRVINE

Distance = 11.5 km = 7 miles

Car Parks: **Troon Harbour Road – Irvine Beach Park**

Walking summary: *Easy* - promenade, pavements, woodland paths,
cycle tracks. Total of 100 m of ascent.

Points of Interest:	
Transport:	Train service
	Good bus service
Historical:	Dundonald Castle. Birthplace of the Stuarts
	Auchans Castle - Admiral Lord Cochrane
	Smuggling associations
	Ancient corn rigs and coppiced woodland
	Edgar Allan Poe
General:	Whinstone quarries
	Fine views of Firth of Clyde
Nature:	Woodland flora and fauna
	SWT Shewalton Wood Reserve
	SWT Gailes Marsh Reserve
	Estuary birds on Bogside mudflats
Eating/Provisions:	Troon Town Centre
	Darley and Loans Shops
	Dundonald Castle Visitor Centre (1 Apr - 31 Oct)
	Dundonald Village Shops
	Irvine Harbourside coffee shops,
	pubs and restaurants
	Irvine Town Centre shops and restaurants
Public toilets:	Dundonald Visitor Centre (1 Apr - 31 Oct)
	Irvine Beach Park
Accommodation:	B&Bs Troon, Loans and Dundonald
	List of Accommodation Irvine Beach Park
	(Check www.ayrshirecoastalpath.org)

Walking: This route is for walkers keen to make the somewhat longer journey of 11.5 miles (19 km) to incorporate a visit via the Smugglers' Trail to the ancient Royal Castle of Dundonald - famous as the birthplace of the Stuart Dynasty of Kings and Queens of Scotland and later - from 1603 - of Great Britain.

Walk along harbour road past Troon Cruising Club and then cut up right on to Templehill, the broad shopping street that leads into Troon Cross. Turn left at the traffic lights along Portland Street, which continues as Dundonald Road and A759 beyond the railway bridge. From here it is a pleasant 2.5 kilometre walk through an attractive area of Troon past Darley Golf Course and out into the flat open countryside that forms a narrow green belt between expanding Troon and the small village of Loans.

Turn left and walk north through Loans on the A759. About 700 m along the road is a sign for the Smugglers' Trail pointing across to a minor road that leads over the A78(T) to a group of cottages. (On the same post is a two-way Coastal Path sign for walkers returning from Dundonald).

During the great smuggling boom of the late 18th century, most of the contraband unloaded from Irish or Manx wherries beached on dark nights on the broad sands of Troon and Gailes beaches, was destined for Loans, and onwards to Dundonald just over the hill. From here, the smuggled goods were distributed by pack pony throughout the county and far beyond. It was smuggling on a grand scale, and hundreds of horses could be mustered when word was passed of the imminent arrival of a large cargo. Import duties at that time on tea, brandy, rum and tobacco were so high that even the wealthy classes who could afford these luxuries were major clients of the smugglers; while among the lower orders, the lower prices of contraband tea and tobacco opened up a big new market.

Excise officers were thin on the ground and poorly supported. They had a thankless task, for even if they did manage to bring a case to court, the likelihood was that the magistrate or judge would have links with the smuggling trade, and the prosecution would fail. Just think, for example, of those caves under Culzean Castle filled with smuggled goods, and recall the wide powers of patronage and 'justice' enjoyed by the Earls of Cassilis, and their aristocratic counterparts in north Ayrshire.

Robert Burns was an excise officer during his time in Dumfries, and in the course of his duties would ride in all weathers up to 200 miles a week through the Dumfries and Kirkcudbright countryside checking inns and taverns for contraband goods. On one occasion, wading chest deep in the Solway, he helped lead a party of dragoons to board the 100-ton smuggling brig *Rosamond*.

The Smugglers' Trail (a round trip of 4.3 km or 3.7 miles from the A759), follows a narrow crooked road past Collennan Farm to a track leading up to the old Troon Reservoir, which is now controlled by Troon Angling Club. There is an excellent Information Board at the start of the path, which climbs up the right side of the dam and runs alongside the reservoir to the Dundonald Woods.

Smugglers Trail - Ancient Rig System

On the south-facing brae-face to the left beyond the reservoir are some fine and rare examples of the old traditional rig system of cultivation, which existed prior to the Agricultural Revolution of the late 18th Century. The raised rigs – or ridges – can still be clearly seen running down the slope, each separated by a shallow furrow. They usually measured about 14 feet across. Soil was scraped from the furrows and heaped into a curved surface to shed excess water and aid drainage. Dung and wrack carted from the beaches would be spread over the surface and ploughed in to nourish soil impoverished by growing the same crops year after year. There was no modern crop rotation. These were the rigs of Robert Burns's time;

> *Corn rigs an' barley rigs,*
> *Corn rigs are bonie:*
> *I'll ne'er forget that happy nicht,*
> *Amang the rigs wi' Annie.*

Burns himself was a farming 'Improver', and successive generations of like-minded Ayrshire farmers since then have ploughed their large fields and gradually obliterated all traces of rigs, except in a few isolated areas like this where grazing was more profitable.

A sense of time-warp continues with interesting old coppiced woodland, probably worked for centuries to provide fuel and timber for the inhabitants of Dundonald and its castle; and ancient moss-covered dykes, which run parallel to the path through a canopy of hazel, alder, ash, oak, beech and sycamore, larch and Scots pine. But beware! In this tranquil setting, walkers might occasionally be startled by loud explosions; for here the path and woodland bisect two huge whinstone quarries - Hillhouse to the north, which covers a huge area of almost half a square kilometre, and Hallyards, 500 metres to the south. But they can relax, for there is no real risk of being bombarded with falling rocks or tumbling over a cliff. Once clear of the quarries, the track winds steeply downhill to emerge beside the Dundonald Burn.

Beyond the burn, cattle timelessly graze the flat water meadows to the south of the impressively strong tower of Dundonald Castle which stands stark and proud on its knoll dominating the village, as it has done for the past 630 years. This is not the first fortification on the site. Sheltered from the prevailing westerly winds, it was first settled in the Stone Age, and held an Iron Age hill fort from 500BC onwards. In the Dark Ages, it was a major stronghold of the old British Kingdom of Strathclyde, which was centred on Dunbarton Rock, and was destroyed about 1000 AD by Angles from Northumbria. The 'Donald' after whom the Dun is named was probably a 10th century king of Strathclyde.

Dundonald Castle

Around 1136, a Norman motte and bailey timber stronghold was erected by Walter Fitzallan, the first Steward to King David I of Scotland. This was replaced in the 13th century by a massive castle built by Alexander Stewart, which subsequently saw the birth of Robert Bruce Stewart - son of Marjorie Bruce and Walter the Steward, and grandson of Robert the Bruce. This castle in turn, was destroyed by the English in the early 14th century.

When Robert Stewart became King Robert II in 1371, he built the present castle to mark his accession to the throne - so Dundonald Castle can truly be said to be the birthplace of the Stuart Dynasty of Kings and Queens of Scotland, and later of Great Britain. This royal line, which included Mary Queen of Scots, James VI and I, Charles I and II, ended finally with Queen Anne.

Recently restored, the Castle and its Visitor Centre are well worth a visit. On the castle forecourt there is a good viewpoint indicator to aid identification of landmarks. The views from the upper windows of the great hall are spectacular. On a clear day the Paps of Jura are visible beyond the top of Arran, Ben Lomond looms to the north, and on the eastern horizon stands the volcanic plug of Loudoun Hill, where the Romans built a camp and signal station, and where Sir William Wallace defeated an English army. In the north middle distance between Dundonald and Irvine lies Shewalton Moss, a flat broad crescent of poorly draining marsh and heath-land extending inland as a raised beach for 4 kilometres without rising more than 20 metres above sea level. This was always poor agricultural land, only used for rough pasture, and over the years a large area has been exploited for sand and gravel extraction, and subsequently for landfill sites. Much of the rest was developed as an industrial zone for Irvine New Town, and contains a surprising number of large and small factories, well screened by woodland.

Dundonald (population 2459) lies below the castle. The traditional village main street of old weavers' cottages leading up to the church has a lot of character and is worth a stroll. The village has increased greatly in recent years with new build homes surrounding its old centre, but remains small enough to retain a good sense of community.

Edgar Allan Poe (1809-1949) the American writer was fostered and lived in Dundonald as a child, after his mother died when he was two years old. His later work may well have been influenced by the towering, dark, haunted ruin on the hill above him.

From the Castle Visitor Centre, an excellent footpath runs west for a kilometre to the ruins of Auchans Castle, built in 1644 for Sir William Cochrane, first Earl of Dundonald. His descendant, later to become the 10th Earl, was Thomas, Admiral Lord Cochrane, one of the Royal Navy's greatest sailors during the Napoleonic Wars; who later founded both the Chilean and Brazilian Navies, and is more famous in South America than in his home country.

In future, it would be superb if the Community Council was able to continue this path past Auchans down the wood-edge dyke to the A759 Kilmarnock road, cross the road and form a woodland then a field-edge path west to the Dundonald roundabout, providing locals with an easy low level cycle/footpath from Dundonald to Troon, while at the same time creating a shorter loop route for walkers wishing to continue north to Irvine.

At present however, this busy A759 is not an option due to the lack of a footpath, and therefore to rejoin the Coastal Path, walkers must retrace their steps from the Visitor Centre back along the Smugglers' Trail to the A759, then turn right along this road for 1 km to the Dundonald roundabout, west of the A78 (T). Here the Path once again links up with the NCN7 on an interesting route through the Shewalton Moss and woodland previously seen from the top of Dundonald Castle.

Follow the NCN7 route under the A78 (T), then across the branch railway line behind the Pulp Mill and along the margins of the Scottish Wildlife Trust's Shewalton Wood Nature Reserve. On either side lies conifer woodland, bordered with scrub birch, alder and willow which grow alongside the deep drainage ditches. The abundant small mammal population attracts predators such as owls, kestrels, buzzards and foxes, and apparently the drier heath-land is home to adders.

The NCN7 leaves the Reserve at its north end, and turns right along Meadowhead Road past the new Meadowhead Sewage Plant. This huge complex treats the combined sewage output of all coastal towns from Ayr to Irvine, and inland to Kilmarnock and beyond, before pumping the purified water along a two-mile sea outfall pipe into Irvine Bay. Over the past few years, it has made a vast difference to the water quality on Ayrshire's bathing beaches. And it doesn't really smell all that bad - even downwind!

Beyond the sewage works, the cycleway turns left and skirts a large water-filled sand and gravel pit that has been left as a wildfowl refuge and coarse fishing facility. A footbridge takes the walker up and over the A78 Irvine Bypass, and suddenly the big skies of that wonderful Firth of Clyde seascape once again dominate the horizon, and the claustrophobic confines of flat, featureless woodland are left behind. The NCN7 now crosses and runs alongside the old Irvine road to the Three Stanes roundabout, from where it follows Marine Drive past the new Gailes leisure and golf complex to the old Gailes farmhouse, sandwiched between the Western and Glasgow Gailes golf courses. There is another small SWT Marsh Reserve off to the left, which is notable for its plant life and butterflies. Once across the railway bridge, the cycleway leaves the road and runs through mixed heath-land and conifer shelterbelts till it reaches the entrance to the Irvine Beach Park cark park.

At this point the Coastal Path diverges from the NCN7. Follow the Coastal Path signs northwest through the large car park to the grassy sward on its seaward side; then climb up to the prominent Dragon Viewpoint and onwards to the Bridge of Scottish Invention and the Magnum Centre.

From the Irvine Beach Park onwards, walkers should revert to the text of **Route 8**.

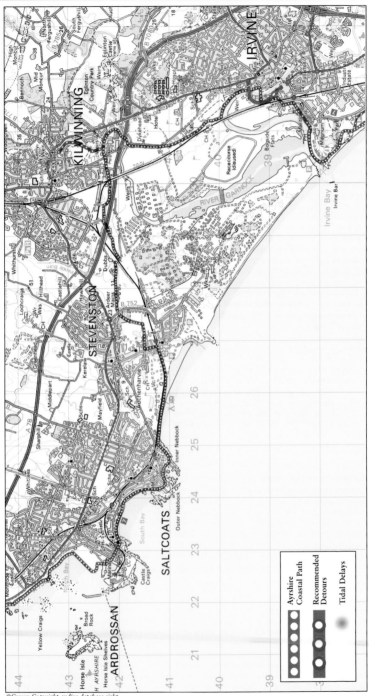

Ayrshire
Coastal Path

Recommended
Detours

Tidal Delays

9. Inland route – IRVINE Low Green - NCN7 north - Town's Moor - Ravenspark - Garnock Floods SWT Nature Reserve - KILWINNING - Kilwinning Abbey - NCN7 south - NCN73 west - Byrehill Road - B752 to Ardeer - Shore Road - STEVENSTON Beach Park - East Shore - Saltcoats Harbour - SALTCOATS South Beach Esplanade - ARDROSSAN Cross, Harbour and Marina

Distance = 17.5 km = 10.8 miles   1/4/11

Car Parks: **Irvine Beach Park – Ardrossan Cross**

Walking summary: *Easy* - promenades, pavements, paths, cycle tracks, minor roads, sandy beaches.

Points of Interest:	
Transport:	Train Services for Ayr, Glasgow, Ardrossan, Largs Good bus services Ferry Terminal for Arran
Historical:	Eglinton Trophy, Cunninghame House, Irvine Cadgers' Racecourse Ardeer Dunes - prehistoric and industrial history Kilwinning Abbey Kilwinning Mother Lodge No 0 Early Industrial Revolution sites, Stevenston and Saltcoats Saltcoats Harbour North Ayrshire Local Museum, Saltcoats Auchenharvie Engine House Ardrossan Castle
General:	Sweeping views of Ayr and Irvine Bays Fine beaches at Stevenston and Saltcoats Ardrossan Harbour and Marina
Nature:	Bogside Flats - ducks and waders SWT Garnock Floods Nature Reserve Stevenston Local Nature Reserve Rivers Irvine and Garnock –Salmon
Eating/Provisions:	Kilwinning shops, pubs and restaurants Saltcoats and Ardrossan seafront shops and hotels
Public Toilets:	Kilwinning Stevenston Beach Park Saltcoats Esplanade
Accommodation:	Hotels and B&Bs, Kilwinning Sandylands Caravan Park, Stevenston Hotels and B&B, Saltcoats and Ardrossan (Check www.ayrshirecoastalpath.org)

Walking: Having returned to the Low Green via Seagate, walk north along the NCW7 cycle path and under the road bridge spanning the River Irvine. From here on, many of the NCN7 signposts include the Ayrshire Coastal Path Logo as the route curves along the riverbank past Irvine's Bicentenary statue of Robert Burns, Just opposite Burns's Statue, is the tidal weir and salmon fish-pass. Four hundred years ago, sailing ships would have come right up the river past this point to load or unload their cargoes at the Low Green and Seagate. There appear to be vestiges of a path, perhaps a towpath, along the outer curve of the riverbank down to the railway bridge.

Beyond the statue lies the Town Moor, and on it, the Cadgers' Racecourse. The Town Moor is still common ground, and in the old days it would be used for grazing and other activities such as racing. Cadgers were itinerant pedlars, or carters, and the Carters' Races with carthorses and ponies still feature prominently on the calendar of the annual Marymas Fair in mid August. The oval racetrack is still well demarcated.

Just across the railway bridge to the south of Bogside Golf Course is the site of Bogside Racecourse, once famous for point-to-point racing and the Scottish Grand National. The course is now disused and the Grand National is run at Ayr. From the railway bridge, walkers will get some idea of the scale of the Ardeer dunes and the broad sweep of the Garnock estuary. The rich feeding on the extensive mudflats between the Irvine and Garnock, known as the Bogside Flats, provides a valuable and nationally important winter refuge for migrant waders, ducks, swans and geese; and each autumn both the Garnock and Irvine rivers also have a good run of salmon.

Garnock Estuary and Bogside Flats

The NCW7 now runs parallel to the railway before veering north alongside the Scottish Wildlife Trust's Garnock Floods Nature Reserve. With its flood plain regularly inundated during autumn and winter, this reserve provides an important wetland sanctuary for duck, geese and waders. Best viewed from the bridge over the Garnock, a short pause here could be rewarding for birdwatchers.

From the Path walkers continue to have good views of the impressive Ardeer Dunes. Out of sight on the seaward side are large primary dunes covered in marram grass, which protect this inland expanse of towering heather-clad, tree-planted, secondary and tertiary dunes, covering over six square kilometres and forming an isolated peninsula between the River Garnock estuary and the sea. So impressive were these dunes in the 18th century that they are described on Captain Armstrong's Map as the 'Ardeer Hills'. Compared with the neighbouring, flat estuarial countryside, they *are* hills - everything is relative!

The wildness and isolation of Ardeer Dunes have proved attractive to man since the Stone Age. The long smooth sandy beach must have been ideal for beaching frail, skin-covered boats; the rivers were full of fish, and the dunes themselves provided shelter for primitive settlements. Thousands of archaeological finds have been made in these dunes and in the surrounding district over the past two centuries, the most important being the recent discovery of a large Bronze Age settlement near the village of Dreghorn about 5 km to the south east of Irvine. This site has just been excavated, and has been hailed as being of major European importance.

Dreghorn has other claims to fame - as the birthplace in 1840 of John Boyd Dunlop – inventor of the pneumatic tyre and one of the names on the Bridge of Scottish Invention; and also as the 18th century village described so vividly in John Galt's *Annals of the Parish*. In more recent history, the remoteness of Ardeer Dunes was a prime factor in 1873, when the Swedish chemist Arthur Nobel decided on a location for his British Dynamite Company Works for the production of nitroglycerine and dynamite. The sand dunes would also absorb and divert skywards most of the shock waves from any disastrous accidental explosion. In addition, there were great commercial advantages for Nobel to site his factory in the United Kingdom, since it gave him access to the greatest market in the world – the British Empire. These Works later became the Nobel Division of Imperial Chemical Industries, and expanded from 100 to 2000 acres, with 20 miles of main railway lines, 75 miles of bogie lines, and 44 miles of water mains on site – the largest explosives factory in the world.

During the war, over 13,000 men and women were employed in the explosives factories. On 7 May 1941, Ardeer ICI Explosives Factory was targeted by the Luftwaffe. Though the first bombs fell short of their target, near Meadowhead and on Bogside racecourse, the factory was hit by 75 bombs, nine of which failed to explode. Twenty buildings were destroyed and many fires started, which were fought by over 30 fire engines. Fortunately, especially for the townsfolk of Irvine, Kilwinning and Stevenston, this attack did not bring about the massive chain reaction, cataclysmic explosion that the Germans had expected. Eight bombs fell on Irvine and 300 incendiary bombs were dropped over Kilwinning, but only six people were killed.

For several years after the War, reaching into the 1950s, over 7,000 workers were still being employed making explosives for industry, with the company gradually diversifying into the production of nitric and sulphuric acid, cellulose, ether, and fertilisers. Later on, the plastics division made nylon.

However, in the 1980s and early 1990s, a major downturn in the world economy forced many multinational companies into a frenzy of rationalisation, contraction and restructuring, with the inevitable and euphemistic 'downsizing,' which in the case of ICI, resulted in massive closures and redundancies. Disastrously for the economy of North Ayrshire, the number of employees at Ardeer was eventually reduced from the wartime high of 13,000 to less than 400. Simultaneous closures of Monsanto Chemicals, coalmines and shipyards left 'The Three Towns' of Stevenston, Saltcoats and Ardrossan in a severely depressed state from which they are only now beginning to recover under the auspices of the Irvine Bay Urban Regeneration Company.

Gazing over the vast empty wilderness of Ardeer Dunes, it must be difficult now for young folk or visitors to Ayrshire to visualise the huge industrial complex with its tall chimneys and massive cooling towers which once dominated the entire landscape; or to comprehend the ever-present sword of Damocles which hung over the townsfolk of Irvine and Stevenston for decades - the possibility of a gigantic explosion at Nobel Division.

After crossing the River Garnock, the Path passes under the A78 and winds upriver along its wooded west bank for 1.5 km to the old town of Kilwinning. In autumn, the pools on this section of river are popular with salmon anglers. Across the river lies Eglinton Country Park and Eglinton Castle, now in ruins as the sad consequence of a spectacular early 19th century example of lordly *'Spend, Spend, Spend'*.

Hugh, 12th Earl of Eglinton, having built the profitable Ardrossan Harbour in 1806 to export coal from his mines (See Page 123), was subsequently left financially high and dry - or sunk - by a half-finished canal, which was planned to run from Glasgow via Johnstone to Ardrossan to link with his harbour. As a result, his successor, Archibald the 13th Earl, inherited debts of several millions of pounds. Sublimely unfazed, and with magnificent recklessness, the bold Earl Archibald then squandered much of what was left of the family fortune on an obscenely extravagant mock-medieval tournament in 1839.

Still talked about today, the famous Eglinton Tournament was held over three days; with a brilliant opening procession of knights in armour accompanied by their ladies, musicians, heralds, squires and jesters, swordsmen and archers - held in a deluge! Like a modern-day Olympics, spectators came from all over Scotland, England and Europe by coach and steamer, on horseback and on foot, to watch the jousting, fencing and archery, and gaze in awe at the cream of Scots and English nobility - and Prince Louis Napoleon of France - in all their lavish finery. After the tournament, 239 of the Earl's friends subscribed to present him with a magnificent silver trophy, four feet high, which took four years to make, and which is now in the safekeeping of North Ayrshire Council and on permanent display to the public at Cunninghame House in Irvine.

But pride cometh before a fall. The Tournament cost £40,000 to stage - about £3.6 million in present-day money - and dragged the Eglinton family fortunes down so low that only 85 years later, the contents of Eglinton Castle had to be auctioned off, and its roof removed to avoid taxation. The castle ruin is now the centrepiece of the 400-acre Eglinton Country Park, which, complete with Visitor Centre, gardens and woodland walks, can be accessed from the NCN7, and is well worth a visit if staying in the district.

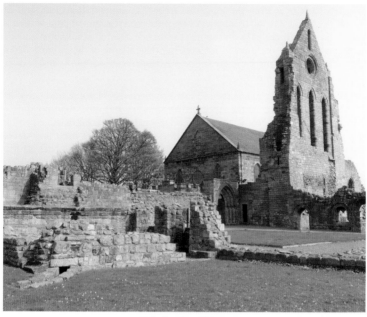

Kilwinning Abbey

Kilwinning (population 15,908) has an ancient history. Its name derives from the Celtic *cil* = monk's cell - of St Winnin, on the site of which was later built a great medieval abbey. The town itself was built at a strategic point where the old Ayr-Irvine-Glasgow road skirted round the top of the Garnock estuary and where the Irvine to Greenock coast road branched west to Ardrossan. The pedestrianised layout of the old town centre incorporates these routes, and although the blight of modern 'planning' has diminished the historical impact of the Abbey and its surrounds, enough remains of the old vernacular buildings to make it pleasantly interesting.

Dating from 1187, the imposing ruins of Kilwinning Abbey still give some impression of its grandeur. Its original twin towers were supported on massive piers larger than those of Westminster Abbey, and in scale, it rivalled Glasgow Cathedral and Paisley Abbey. Like so many other abbeys, it was destroyed in the 16th century during the Scottish Protestant Reformation. The chancel remained as the local Presbyterian parish kirk until it was replaced by the present, simple, unadorned Abbey Church in the late 18th century.

When the great north-west tower of the Abbey fell down in 1814, the Kilwinning Archers - formed in 1483 - were deprived of a platform for their centuries-old Papingo Shoot. This ancient tradition had its origins in a 13th century Royal decree which directed all the nobility and their retainers to hold a periodic show of weapons - or *wapenshaw*. The Earl of Eglinton's followers tested their archery skills by the distinctly dodgy practice of shooting vertically upwards at a wooden parrot or papingo (English = popinjay), sticking out from the top of the old tower. When gunpowder and

115

muskets took over from the longbow, archery continued as a sport, and in 1724, the Silver Arrow Trophy was first presented for annual competition - which lasted 150 years. In due course the archers used a 'new' Abbey tower, which was quickly built in 1815, soon after the collapse of the original. After a gap of 78 years, the Papingo Shoot was resurrected in 1948, and is now held each year in June.

Kilwinning's other main claim to fame concerns its Masonic traditions. In the Main Street near to the Abbey ruins stands a red sandstone building - Mother Kilwinning No. 0 Masonic Lodge - generally acknowledged to be the first Masonic Lodge in Scotland. Although the building itself only dates from 1883, the original Masonic connections must have gone back to the building of the Abbey itself.

To move on to Ardrossan, walkers should now retrace their steps for about 1 km back along the Garnock to join the NCN73, which runs through an industrial estate to join Byrehill Road and pass under the A78 at Todhill Farm.

As this is an access road to several farms, a look out should be kept for cars and vans as well as bikes and horses. Beyond Todhill Training Centre, good views can be had of the 'Ardeer Hills' across low-lying water meadows. Continue under the railway and past the caravan park and Ardeer Mains to the B732. Cross this road to enter Ardeer Park, through which a pleasant path edges past the miniature golf course and runs along an old earthwork dam - which may have been part of the original canal system carrying Robert Reid Cunninghame's coal to Saltcoats Harbour (see below). Passing an ornamental loch, the NCN73 joins New Street in **Stevenston.**

On travelling along this street past the railway station, once over the level crossing the NCN73 bears right and runs parallel to the railway line for 1.5km, while the Coastal Path carries straight on down Shore Road to reach the west end of Stevenston Beach Park. The strange grey shoreline rock on Stevenston Beach Park promontory just to the east is iron slag, since much of the Beach Park was reclaimed from a huge unsightly slag bing, the product of an iron works built near the Ardeer coal pits in the 19th century.

Stevenston (population 9129) itself lies awkwardly inland, separated from the sea by the main railway line. Originally a medieval parish with a church and small agricultural village on the road from Kilwinning Abbey to Saltcoats, it was named after Stephen Loccard, the son of a Norman who was granted the barony in the 11th century. It grew in importance, along with Saltcoats, as local landed proprietors began to exploit the mineral wealth of their coal and iron measures. Just before the opening of the Nobel Works, Stevenston had reached a population of 5,000, and in the hundred years which followed, it rose to 14,000 as the town and district prospered.

Now slowly recovering from industrial closures, major land reclamation projects have removed almost all traces of those former industries, and given Stevenston a pride in several fine areas of parkland including the Beach Park, over which it is a pleasant change to be able to walk on firm turf and along a tarmac path skirting East Shore Sands. Beyond the west car park is a new metal footbridge over the Stevenston Burn leading walkers on to a fine sandy beach edged by the dunes of the Stevenston local nature reserve.

December squall over Stevenston Beach

At one point on the edge of the beach, observant walkers should note the low eroded remnants of an ancient pit bing, a jumbled mixture of shale, sandstone slabs, and mudstone, with a small section of red blaes where at one time residual coal in the bing must have caught fire due to spontaneous combustion. This spoil heap may look insignificant, but it is an important reminder of the dawn of the Industrial Revolution – 250 to 300 years ago - in the west of Scotland. It is humbling to think that - as well as the valuable coal - this waste spoil would have been be drawn to the pit bottom on wooden sleds, raised to the surface in creels by horse-drawn windlasses, and finally tipped from wooden hutches on to the shore - often hauled by boys as young as ten.

200 year old burning bing

Saltcoats (population 11260) developed as a small fishing village between the two medieval parishes of Stevenston and Ardrossan. It took its name *Salt-cotts* from the cot-houses of the folk involved in evaporating salt from seawater to provide salt for the curing of fish. Initially done on a small scale using surface coal, this all changed when deep coal measures were discovered, and the Cunninghames of Auchenharvie built huge coal-fired seawater vats near the harbour - and made their fortune exporting both coal and salt.

By unfortunately straddling the boundary between the powerful estates of the Montgomeries of Eglinton who owned Ardrossan Castle, and the Cunninghames of Glencairn whose estates included Stevenston, the poor inhabitants of Saltcoats were frequently embroiled in the territorial bickerings of their feudal lordships. To safeguard his rights following yet another of those Ayrshire baronial feuds, the Earl of Eglinton obtained the promise of a Burgh Charter from James V in 1528 for the Ardrossan side of Saltcoats, while the Earl of Glencairn took legal steps to protect his end of the town, where the fishing industry and his coal mines were concentrated.

While small bell pits had been sunk around Saltcoats before 1680 by his great-grandfather who constructed the first harbour in 1684 to export his coal, it was from 1770 onwards that the ruthless entrepreneurial skills of Robert Reid Cunninghame of Auchenharvie began to develop the North Ayrshire coalfields well before the rest of the county. In 1772 he dug a 2-mile canal to transport coal to Saltcoats harbour. Later, crippled in 1812 by turnpike tolls on his carts - which carried 42,000 tons of coal per year over Eglinton land - he was forced to build a horse-drawn railway (copied from that of the Duke of Portland at Troon) to bypass their toll road on land he had reclaimed from the sea.

Winter waves at Saltcoats

The Path now follows this route along the modern sea wall to the harbour. *In southwesterly gales the sea wall takes a severe pounding from huge waves, and anyone daft enough to be walking along this stretch under such conditions should take great care.*

Before visiting the harbour, walkers who may be interested can make a small 500-metre detour inland along Saltcoats Road to Auchenharvie Park, to enjoy the park and see the ruined engine house for Auchenharvie Colliery, whose great Newcomen beam engine was used to pump water from the workings in the late 18th century. It was not uncommon near the coast, to lose pits to an influx of seawater.

While Ayrshire landed proprietors made their fortunes, the conditions endured by their workers were atrocious. Colliers were still bound to their pit by law and could not leave without permission of the owners. They worked by candlelight, sometimes waist deep in water. Pick-men or hewers could earn one pound for a six-day week, while pit-head men earned 9 shillings a week. But compared with the six pounds per half year earned by agricultural labourers, this was 'big money', and explained why boys, men and women left the countryside in droves to risk their lives down coal pits. Life was short and dangerous as a pick-man underground.

Saltcoats Harbour

Life at sea could be tough as well - especially for a woman! Betsy Miller was born in Saltcoats in 1793, the daughter of a sea captain trading out of Saltcoats harbour with his two-masted brig, the *Clytus*. His daughter was interested in sailing and was allowed to accompany her father from the age of fifteen and became proficient in seamanship and navigation. When her father died ten years later, leaving large debts, Betsy got the reluctant approval of her mother to take command of the *Clytus*, and became the first woman ever to be recorded as a ship's captain in the British Register of Tonnage at Lloyds. An amazing woman, she spent over 50 years shipping coal and limestone between Ayrshire ports and Ireland, and finally retired at the age of sixty-nine.

It is difficult to imagine the small L-shaped drying harbour at Saltcoats as being able to export coal, but it could handle ships from 20 to 200 tons and up to 24 vessels at a time - albeit slowly, with delays in loading and discharging cargo. The main exports were coal, salt, and textiles from the local handloom weavers; with imports of fish from Newfoundland, the northern Highlands and Clyde, and also grain. The seaward extension was built in 1847, when there were about thirty ships exporting coal, stone, herring and woollen textiles; and importing herring from the Clyde and oats from Ireland. Shipbuilding and rope-works also flourished here until the completion of Ardrossan's deep-water harbour in 1810. Built by

Cunninghame's equally ruthless rival and traditional enemy - Hugh, 12th Earl of Eglinton - for his own coal exports, this development drew trade away from Saltcoats and, together with the collapse of handloom weaving, heralded the industrial failure of the burgh.

It was not until the late 19th century that Saltcoats fortunes revived with the Victorian fashion for seaside holidays, and this phase of the town's history is very evident in the fine Victorian villas that look over the equally fine sands of the South Beach. Just north of the harbour, beyond the promontory, are three seawater bathing pools of various depths on a flat natural sandstone base, which once were very popular, but which are no longer used by the young 'softies' of today, who prefer the comforts of the heated indoor pool at Auchenharvie Sports Centre. The rough shoreline round the point provides a good habitat for waders such as Turnstone, Redshank, and Oystercatcher, which can be seen busily and unobtrusively feeding among the rocks at quite close quarters, seemingly unconcerned by the presence of casual passers-by.

South Beach is a broad expanse of clean, well-manicured yellow sand, bordered by a wide esplanade, complete with attractive floral displays, bandstands and an interesting large sundial - set at 'Saltcoats Local Time' - which is important for any walkers trying to synchronise their watches to catch the Arran ferry! Halfway along, at the point where the Stanley Burn emerges from the seawall, the walker has crossed the burgh border into Ardrossan.

Ardrossan (population 10952) is built on the site of a very ancient settlement. The name came later - from the Gaelic *ard-rossan* - 'the point of the jutting out ridge', which aptly describes the low spur behind the fine villas of South Crescent Road on which stands what is left of Ardrossan Castle. At the base of the ridge was discovered a large shell mound or midden of Stone Age hunter-gatherers, containing the bones of oxen, red deer, goat, pig, horse, grouse, puffin, conger eel and beaver, and shells now extinct in the Clyde. The strategic importance of this small hillock was obviously attractive to man for thousands of years before the Celts and their Norman successors. On the seaward side of South Crescent road, opposite the Barony Church, stands the War Memorial, a tall Celtic Cross. Nearby is another memorial to wartime casualties closer to home - a large granite boulder with a plaque inscribed: *This memorial is dedicated to the officers and men who perished when HMS Dasher, an Archer class aircraft carrier, sank on 27th March 1943. "We will remember them"*.

An American-built ship, the *Dasher* had been taking part in exercises about halfway between Ardrossan and Arran when she suddenly exploded and sank in a few minutes, with the loss of 379 officers and men. The exact cause of the explosion remains unclear, but it is thought to have been due to the ignition of fuel vapour.

Another mysterious event occurred in the aftermath of the tragedy, which has only recently come to light as a result of researches by John Steele, a local man who has written a book on *The Secrets of HMS Dasher*. In the 1956 film *The Man Who Never Was,* British Military Intelligence dressed a man's body in a major's uniform and dumped him from a submarine off the coast of Spain, with a briefcase handcuffed to his wrist. Inside were battle plans detailing an Allied invasion of Greece. Designed to draw German divisions to Greece while the Allies prepared for the invasion of Sicily, the hoax worked when, as expected, the Major's body was handed over to the Germans by the Spanish authorities. That man, who in death probably saved the lives of countless others following that invasion, was called John Melville. Though there is a grave in Ardrossan War Cemetery marked 'John Melville', it is claimed that it was his body - that of a recently drowned man - which was taken away by the authorities and used in the famous hoax.

From the west end of South Crescent Road, Princes Street leads over a level crossing and on to Ardrossan Cross. By taking a short detour along Bute Place, an unprepossessing industrial street on the right just before the Cross, access can be gained to the Castle Hill up a series of steps. The large obelisk at the top was erected by the townsfolk in 1849 to commemorate Alexander McFadzean Esq., M.D. who was held *'in high esteem for his active benevolence in the exercise of his profession'* - and also for his endeavours to have Ardrossan created a burgh.

The splendid view from the top gives some idea of the simple grid plan layout of Ardrossan itself, drawn up for the Earl of Eglinton who developed his model town at the same time as he was constructing the harbour in 1805. There is a fine distant prospect from south to north over the Firth of Clyde, but sadly much of the foreground is taken up with small industrial premises and areas of dereliction. Over towards the harbour however, there are encouraging signs of regeneration with a major harbourside house-building development on old dockland and the site of the former Shell oil depot.

The Castle itself is badly neglected and vandalised with graffiti and discarded beer cans - which is disappointing, given its ancient history. Dating probably from the 13th Century, it was occupied by the English, and attacked and taken by Sir William Wallace during his campaign. Subterfuge was used to entice the garrison out to extinguish a nearby house on fire, following which, according to the historian Pont, *'he gave them a very hot welcome, killed every mother's son, and forthwith forced the castle and won it'*. Their bodies he threw into a vault - thereafter known as Wallace's Larder. In its prime as a Montgomerie stronghold, Ardrossan was a powerful fortress on a par with Turnberry, Dunure, and Dundonald Castles.

Later it became literally, 'just one of those ruins that Cromwell knocked about a bit', when in 1652, Oliver Cromwell used it as a quarry and shipped much of the stonework down to Ayr to build the Citadel - thus destroying the power base of Hugh, son and heir to the Earl of Eglinton, who had fought as a Royalist at the Battle of Worcester and as a result had his estates forfeited. Only the tower keep, a vaulted kitchen and two cellars remain.

The Eglintons had the last laugh however, when Charles II was restored to the throne, and in a tit-for-tat, granted to them the Citadel of Ayr and all its grounds, which had been possessed by the 'late usurpers'. (To this day from within the Fort district of Ayr, the grand Montgomerie and Eglinton Terraces both look down on lowly Cromwell Road - a rather narrow wynd outwith the ramparts.)

A zig-zag path down the north west slope brings the walker to Glasgow Street where a left turn leads back to Ardrossan Cross, the Harbour and the Marina.

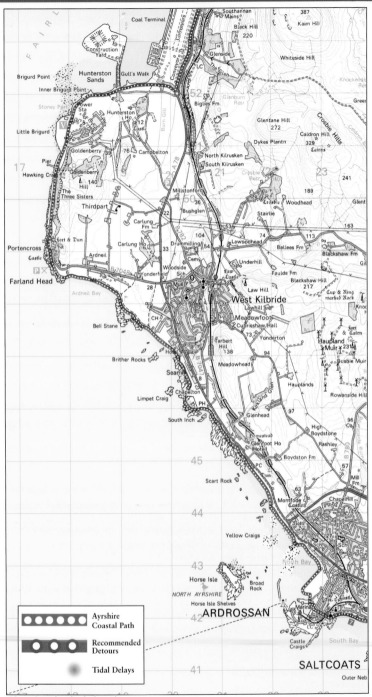

Ayrshire
Coastal Path

Recommended
Detours

Tidal Delays

122

10. ARDROSSAN Harbour and Marina - North Beach - SEAMILL - PORTENCROSS

Distance = **10.5 km = 6.5 miles** *+ 2.4 to get bus !* *8/4/11*

Car Parks: **Ardrossan Cross – Portencross Car Park**

Walking summary: *Easy* - promenades, pavements, paths, cycle tracks, sandy beaches.

Points of Interest:	
Transport:	Train Services for Largs, Ayr, Glasgow Good bus services Ferry Terminal for Arran
Historical:	Ardrossan Harbour Iron Age duns on escarpment Ancient fish cruives or traps The Sea Mill
General:	Ardrossan Harbour and Marina Photogenic coastline West Kilbride Craft Town
Nature:	Coastal birds and seals Coastal geology
Eating/Provisions:	Rowan Tree roadside restaurant Waterside Inn Seamill and West Kilbride shops
Public Toilets:	A78 at north entrance to Ardrossan Boydston Shore
Accommodation:	Hotels and B&Bs in Ardrossan Hotels and B&Bs in Seamill (Check www.ayrshirecoastalpath.org)

The Harbour: From Ardrossan Cross the road curves round to the Harbour Station and the Ferry Terminal. Ardrossan Harbour has evolved and changed a lot since its original development by the 12th Earl of Eglinton in 1805 for his coal and ironstone exports. The long curved outer pier was built in two years, but it was not until 1839 that plans for a large wet dock were implemented, complete with dry dock and shipbuilding facilities that were in use for the next 135 years. In addition to coal, as the shipping trade developed, exports grew to include steel, oil, petroleum and asphalt. The main imports were iron ore, limestone, oil, petrol, scrap metal and timber. Passenger ferry services ran from Ardrossan to Isle of Man, Belfast and Arran. The harbour was so busy that for many years, two railway companies each had their own station on the pier. One station still operates. Sadly, the shipyard, and oil terminal have gone. Only the vital Arran ferry service remains. The short eight-mile crossing to Brodick only takes 40 minutes and the ferry runs every two hours. As this service expanded and ships progressively increased in size, the wet dock was in-filled in 1984 to provide space for a new Ferry Terminal. The large inner harbour is now divided in two by a dock-gate, with the inner part converted recently into the Clyde Marina.

Ardrossan Marina

Clydeport, the Ardrossan Harbour's owners, and North Ayrshire Council have ambitious plans to re-develop its derelict dockside and adjacent industrial sites. An Asda supermarket was completed in 2007, and luxury private apartments with a wonderful view up the Firth of Clyde have already been built around the marina, with the next phase under construction. An even larger housing development is scheduled over the next few years for the old Shell depot site in conjunction with the building of a new breakwater to enclose a second marina for 360 yachts in the Shell tanker basin.

To the west beyond the outer breakwater in North Bay lies the long low outline of Horse Island, which provides shelter to the bay and harbour from northwesterly gales. Negotiating the entrance and docking can be difficult in southwesterly gales, sometimes forcing the ferry to use the pier at Wemyss Bay as an alternative. Horse Island is said to get its name from its use as a

Winter Arran from Ardrossan

place of quarantine for imported horses. Many ships have foundered on the reefs surrounding the island, and the large pyramidal structure at its south end is a 52-foot landmark beacon erected there by the Earl of Eglinton in 1811. Horse Island is now a seabird nature reserve administered by the RSPB.

Walking: From the Cross, the Path follows a wide public promenade round the Marina, passes between the apartment blocks, and continues round the square basin used in the past by tankers unloading at the now-demolished Shell oil depot. Since the housing development and beach promenade round North Bay is not scheduled to be completed for 3-5 years from 2007, Clydeport have kindly agreed to consider providing a temporary shoreline path round the bay for use by local and visiting walkers before and during the construction phase.

Snow on Arran from Ardrossan

On reaching the top of the bay, walkers now have the option of using the asphalt path alongside the modern A78 coast road to Greenock or simply wandering along the beach to Seamill. As in parts of South Ayrshire, this latter route follows the old 18th century coast road on Armstrong's Map, which ran along much of the beach from Ardrossan to Chapelton, and is by far the better option.

Along Boydston Shore, the sand is fairly firm underfoot, and the noise of busy traffic on the A78T is almost imperceptible from the tide line. Occasionally it might be necessary to divert on to the roadside path if any of the easily fordable small burns is in spate. The sand has an attractive pinkish rosy glow in the sunlight due to its origins in the extensive old red sandstone outcrops, reefs and drying rocks which make this stretch of coastline so photogenic when the tide is out. Look out for several igneous dykes thrusting though fissures in the sandstone, and one in particular near Seamill where what looks like a drystane dyke has been built at an angle along the sandstone bedrock to form a V with the natural dyke. This is probably the remnant of an ancient fish cruive used to maroon and trap fish as the tide receded.

Boydston Shore to Seamill

Erected in 2004, the clutter of massive wind generators dominating the hillside above Ardrossan fortunately disappear behind the tree-clad slopes of the raised beach escarpment - and from the consciousness of the walker - with only the occasional flicker of a white blade tip to show that they are busy and quietly competing with Hunterston B nuclear power station five miles up the coast. On the escarpment near Boydston Farm is an Iron Age dun, and half way to Seamill, at the foot of the slope lies Glenfoot House, for many years the corporate entertainment facility of ICI Ardeer, and now a hotel. Above it, in the woods, is a homestead from more ancient times. Buzzards can be seen, hanging stiff-winged and motionless in the updraught above the escarpment, scanning the fields of the raised beach below for rabbits or voles. There are a number of popular car parks with picnic facilities along the roadside for any fastidious walkers disinclined to munch sand with their sandwiches.

About a kilometre further on, the Path follows the curve of a pink-tinged beach out to South Inch point, by-passing the caravan park and pub and continuing north along the beach on a well-defined track till level with Chapelton and the farm-like buildings of Seamill's sewage pump station. From here a broad, designated footpath runs along the track of the underground sewage pipe between seaside bungalows and the foreshore to the foot of Kilbride Burn, which runs into the sea next to Seamill Hydro. The footbridge over the burn provides a good view upstream of the original Sea Mill, from which **Seamill** takes its name. Dating from around 1790, it still retains its old millwheel. On the landward side of the main road is the site of another ancient fort.

Ayrshire tattie field

Seamill is essentially an outlying coastal suburb of the much larger village of West Kilbride (population 4393) which lies inland, wedged between the A78 and the Kilbride Burn, partly hidden and strangely detached from the world passing by on the main road. West Kilbride has recently re-invented itself as a 'Craft Town', with a number of craft shops and galleries worth a visit. Otherwise, it is by and large, a fairly affluent and desirable dormitory town, with most folk travelling to work while still enjoying all the amenities of fresh sea air, a fine beach and splendid golf course nearby.

Seamill Hydro Hotel originated in 1871 as a hydropathic spa, but has evolved and extended to incorporate a leisure club and conference facilities, and is often used as a pre-match retreat by the Scottish football team. Its extensive gardens and tennis courts extend to the shoreline and are protected from the elements by a high seawall. Walking along the sand beneath the wall is pleasant, and beyond the hotel a stroll up Hyndman Road gives access to the village across the A78T. For vehicles, Hyndman Road also provides access to an open grassy area and car park beside the beach.

Raised above the beach to the north of this park, a good, metalled path runs parallel to Seamill Golf Course for two kilometres to the far end of Ardneil Bay and the aptly named Farland Head, giving fine views of the fort and dun on Auld Hill above Portencross, the Wee Cumbrae and Garroch Head at the south end of Bute. Bisecting the beach in the foreground are the Bastion Craig and the Bell Stane - two impressive outcrops of old red sandstone.

The Path then peters out for the last couple of hundred yards over a shingle beach, till the walker comes to a new metal kissing gate, which accesses a well-trodden track bordering the arable fields round Farland Head to a second metal kissing gate next to Portencross car park.

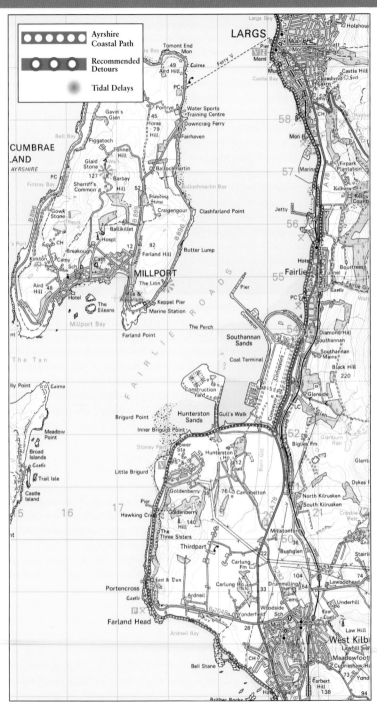

11. PORTENCROSS Castle - Three Sisters - Hunterston Nuclear Power Station - Hunterston Sands - Gull's Walk - A78 Cycle Path - FAIRLIE Shore Path - Fairlie Church - Fairlie Marina Bridge - Causeway Walk - LARGS Marina

21/4/11

Distance = **11.5 km = 7.1 miles**

Car Parks: **Portencross Car Park – Largs Marina public car park**

Walking summary: *Easy* – farm tracks, pavements, paths, cycle tracks.

Points of Interest:	
Transport:	Train service from Largs to Ayr and Glasgow Good bus service Ferry to Great Cumbrae
Historical:	Portencross hill fort and dun Portencross Castle and Spanish Galleon The Hawking Craig Hunterston Castle Southannan House Fairlie Castle Fife of Fairlie Yachts Kelburn Castle
General:	Portencross harbours The Three Sisters Hunterston Nuclear Power Stations Hunterston Construction Yard Clyde Port Deepwater Terminal Largs Marina
Nature:	Birds of prey, shore and sea birds Coastal geology Natural woodlands Waders and ducks on Hunterston Flats
Eating/Provisions:	Fairlie shops Largs Yacht Haven
Public Toilets:	Burnfoot Picnic Park, Fairlie
Accommodation:	List of Accommodation, Fairlie Picnic Park (Check www.ayrshirecoastalpath.org)

Walking: From the picnic area and car park, it is only a short distance to the medieval peel tower of Portencross Castle. Although the lands of the Barony of Ardneil were granted to Sir Robert Boyd of Kilmarnock by Robert the Bruce, for his staunch support before Bruce was hunted into exile in 1306, the castle itself was not built until the reign of Robert II, around 1371. Built on a shallow promontory of steeply inclined old red sandstone strata, it is a modest four storeys high and remained occupied until 1739 when the roof was blown off in a violent storm. Despite this, the castle remains in a very good state of preservation, and featured in the BBC series 'Restoration 2004' - though unfortunately it was not selected as a finalist in the competition for a restoration grant. Snuggled below its east wall is a tiny natural harbour, complemented by a larger one a hundred metres to the north; both still occupied by a few small pleasure craft, which add to the picturesque atmosphere of this hidden corner of North Ayrshire.

Portencross Castle

Farland Head and Portencross were at one time small fishing communities, but the Castle and its strategic coastal situation were of much greater importance in ancient times. Prominent on Auld Hill just above the Castle is a much earlier Iron Age hill fort and dun. Prior to the Norman conquest, it was from Portencross that the bodies of the ancient Scottish kings sailed on their last journey to be buried on Iona. Their actual route is not described. Presumably the galleys would have sailed round Garroch Head on Bute, and up Loch Fyne to Tarbert, where after a short land crossing, the bier would have been transferred to another galley on the west side of Kintyre for the sea voyage through the Sound of Islay, and past Colonsay to Iona. Otherwise, they would have had to face an extremely long and exposed passage down the Firth of Clyde, brave the treacherous waters of the Mull of Kintyre, and endure an equally long voyage back up the Kintyre coast - as any modern-day yacht skipper from Largs marina will confirm!

When the present Castle was built - conveniently halfway between his royal castles of Dundonald and Rothesay - Robert II stayed there on frequent occasions. Two centuries later, in 1588, one of the Spanish galleons that had fled from Sir Francis Drake's fleet by sailing up the North Sea and down the west coast of Scotland to get back to Spain, sank just off Portencross in a storm. Seventeen of the crew survived. The wreck was discovered in 1740, and several cannon were recovered. One apparently sat in front of the castle for many years, but disappointingly it is now in very poor condition and is no longer there.

A good farm track follows the shoreline past the cottages and harbour, giving wonderful views across the Hunterston Channel and Fairlie Roads to the Wee Cumbrae with its own miniature castle - and further north, to the Big Cumbrae and the town houses of the small seaside resort of Millport tightly congregated round its bay. The Wee Cumbrae is privately owned and not easily accessible, but friendly Big Cumbrae is very popular with holiday visitors, and day-trippers wishing to walk or cycle the 16 km (10 miles) round its delightful coastline.

Passing by a small, disued concrete pier, the track curves round a rocky outcrop and emerges through a gate on to arable land on the raised beach. *In autumn and winter, this is used for grazing sheep and the gate must be kept closed.* To the right is Ardneil Hill with its mile-long rampart of impressive sandstone cliffs. The central group of spectacular rock buttresses is known as The Three Sisters, and the most northerly bluff is called The Hawking Craig, proclaiming the fact that for centuries this has been an ideal habitat for buzzard, peregrine and raven, and was in all certainty, the supply source for the Hunters of Hunterston, of young peregrines for the royal falconry. The lower slopes are clad in thick natural woodland, mainly ash, hawthorn, oak, beech and sycamore.

A huge man-made glass cliff peeping out incongruously from beyond the Hawking Craig soon reveals itself as the first of two Magnox reactor buildings of Hunterston A Nuclear Power Station - which started generating in 1960. It was during the early sixties that a unique and innovative new technology was developed, whereby Hunterston's surplus night-time production of cheap electricity was utilised in faraway Argyll to pump water from Loch Awe through vertical shafts to a storage dam a thousand feet up Ben Cruachan. During peak daytime demand for electricity, the flow was reversed and water rushed downhill to drive the turbines of a giant generating station built deep in the heart of the mountain. Decommissioned in 1990, all the uranium rods have long since been removed from the reactor cores, and work is going on at present to provide long-term storage facilities on site for intermediate nuclear waste.

Next-door is the equally huge monolithic building housing the advanced gas-cooled reactors of Hunterston B Nuclear Power Station, which was opened in 1976 and which supplies 25 per cent of Scotland's electricity. There is a Visitor Centre, and guided tours of the plant can be arranged.

At low tide, while strolling along the pavement beside the public road that runs past the power station and curves round the shoreline of Hunterston Sands, walkers will gain some idea of the huge expanse of tidal flats which existed here before the area was industrialised. Covering an area of almost 5 square kilometres, Hunterston and Southannan Sands provided one of the most important Scottish winter feeding grounds for immense flocks of duck, waders and sea birds; and the panoramic view from Fairlie shore was arguably one of the finest and most unspoiled in Scotland. Despite long and vigorous protests from the local community and environmentalists, the construction of Hunterston deepwater ore terminal was given the go ahead in the late 1970s - primarily to supply Ravenscraig Steelworks in Lanarkshire with iron ore. Simultaneously, to the south west of the massive pier - which can accommodate bulk carriers up to 300,000 tonnes - a huge square hole was excavated for the purpose of constructing oilrigs.

Almost predictably, within a few years, Ravenscraig was closed and, like that other famous Firth of Clyde hole in the ground into which millions of pounds of public money was poured - at Portavadie on Loch Fyne - the Hunterston Construction Yard has remained unused and derelict for many years since its last commission - a huge floating dry dock for the nuclear submarines at Faslane. Thankfully, an earlier, almost Soviet-style plan - to establish a giant steelworks beside the ore terminal on this beautiful piece of coastline - was eventually dropped!

The ore terminal has now been converted to unload coal for UK power stations - from faraway countries like Australia, Poland and Colombia - and there is a plan under serious consideration at present, to develop a major European hub container terminal at Hunterston. Whether this will simply utilise the huge derelict construction site, or result in yet even more of the sands being destroyed, remains to be seen.

Opposite Hunterston House, built in the late 18th century, the Path now forsakes a busy power station thoroughfare and passes between metal gates to join the quiet unused public road built to serve the construction yard. The Hunter family, who were hereditary keepers of the king's hunting forests on Arran, have been in continuous occupation of the Lands of Hunterston for over 800 years. With their former magnificent views of the Cumbrae, Largs and the Cowal Hills now ruined by giant cranes and derelict yards, one wonders if the present-day Hunters ever regret their ancestors' decision to leave the ancient castle tucked behind woodland just a few hundred yards inland.

It is worthwhile making a small 600 metre detour south along the cycle route to have a wee look at Hunterston Castle. Built in the 14th Century, it is a delightful miniature castle, whose small peel tower still retains its original rafters and roof trusses, complete with carpenters' adze marks.

As the seat of the Hunter Clan, it is open only to Clan members, except for 'Open Doors Day' each year when its doors are open for one day to the general public. For those lucky enough to gain admission, pride of place is given to a replica of the famous Hunterston Brooch, a large silver Celtic brooch dating from around 700 AD, overlaid with fine gold filigree work, and set with amber stones. Found in 1826 by a two ditch diggers working at the foot of the Hawking Craig, the original is now in the Scottish National Museum in Edinburgh, and is regarded as probably the finest piece of Celtic craftsmanship ever discovered in Scotland.

Deep Water Terminal - Fairlie

On reaching the A78 roundabout, straddled by a hideous huge blue covered conveyor which reaches up to the railway on the hill, the Path now follows an NCN cycle track north to Fairlie. This 2 km stretch is not as bad as it first seems, for the path meanders through planted woodland well back from the road for much of the way; and in early Autumn provides a non-stop feast of black, juicy brambles. Later on, it must also be a fine place for avian berry-feeders such as blackbirds, fieldfares and redwings, since much of the sensitive landscaping between the road and the ore terminal incorporates berry-bearing trees such as gean, rowan, whitebeam, crab apple, and sea buckthorn. And talking of food, with the wind in the right (-or wrong!) direction, walkers themselves may be driven into a feeding frenzy by the delicious smells emanating from the Fence Bay Smokery and seafood restaurant on the other side of the road.

Hidden in the woods opposite the entrance to the Clydeport Ore Terminal, sits Southannan House, in the older castle part of which, Mary Queen of Scots and her entourage slept one night in July 1563 on her pilgrimage south to Whithorn Priory. Also hidden - behind the landscaping north of the roundabout - is a large lagoon, built as a wildfowl refuge on what remained of Southannan and Hunterston Sands after the terminal was built. Encircled by a railway line, it is protected from disturbance by the public.

Fairlie (population 1510). A few hundred metres on, the Path arrives at Fairlie and veers left to a picnic area on the small promontory at Burnfoot - an ideal spot at which to rest and absorb the fine view north past Fairlie village to Largs, and beyond to the Cowal hills above Dunoon. Many yachts lie on traditional moorings in Fairlie Bay, and one positive benefit from the ore terminal is that they are now much more sheltered from south-westerly gales. Energetic 'castle collectors' might wish to detour 200 metres along the main road, then follow Fairlie Burn uphill for 500 metres to the well-

Winter morning - Fairlie

133

preserved early 16th century tower of Fairlie Castle, once owned by the Boyles of Kelburn. Beyond this is a fine walk up Fairlie Glen past a series of waterfalls and into the hills.

Set against a garden wall next to the picnic area, is a very old milestone. On one side, barely decipherable, it reads Largs 3 Greenock 17 ; and on the other it has Irvine 16 Kilwinning 13. This milestone is a relic of the old Shore Road, which once was the main route past the village, and the course of which the Path now follows.

In 1842, Lord Cockburn wrote : *Fairlie is the best village of the wealthy in Scotland. Excellent houses, capital gardens, umbragueous trees, the glorious Clyde, backed by Arran and its dependencies stretched out before them, a gravelly solid, and a mild western climate.*

This praise of Fairlie's qualities - which is still appropriate in 2004 - explains just why so little now remains of the old Shore Road. During the mid-1800s, it was swallowed up by high seawalls guarding the extended properties of wealthy industrialists who were able to commute to Glasgow by steamer from the new pier at Largs. Of the humble North, Mid (or Ferry) and South Rows which comprised 18th century Fairlie, only Ferry Row remains today. Formerly thatched, single-storied fisher and ferry men's cottages, but now two-storied, they also over the years have extended their frontages to include most of the road which once ran in front of them. Here it is worth a pause to stand and stare, blank out the pier and cranes, and appreciate just how beautiful the view must have been until the 1960s - and, to a certain extent, still is. *At the top of high spring tides, walkers unable to scramble over rocks might find it safer to make a detour up on to the main road and follow it along to Fairlie Parish Church.*

Skirting the seawall, the shore path continues over a mixture of sand, shingle, and sandstone to the jetty below Bay Street, where there is an option either to follow Bay Street up to the Parish Church on the main road, or to continue on a slightly longer route along the sandy beach to a second picnic area on the site of the old railway pier (built 1882), and then double back to the Parish Church. The second option takes walkers past an attractive modern development on the site of the famous Fife of Fairlie Boatyard. Established in 1770 by William Fife, many famous racing yachts - including Sir Thomas Lipton's America's Cup contender *Shamrock*, and the Marquis of Ailsa's all-conquering *Bloodhound* - were designed or built here until the start of the Second World War in 1939.

In 1998, and again in 2003, a large number of these magnificent 70-90 year-old yachts - many owned by millionaire enthusiasts - gathered at Largs from all over the world for a Fife Regatta. The televised spectacle of supremely elegant racing yachts creaming along under full sail as they beat round the Cumbraes, re-enacted those glorious days of Empire when the upper Firth of Clyde vied with Cowes as the yachting mecca of Edwardian Britain.

A word of warning, the church-like brick building situated behind the picnic tables on the old pier is not what it seems - it is the Fairlie Waste Water Treatment Works! Its designers must have been very confident of its efficiency - and with some justification - since there is not a hint of odour upwind or downwind, and the picnic area seems well frequented.

Fife Regatta - Largs June 1998

From one ecclesiastic building to another - the road from the pier now leads to Fairlie Parish Church, whose spire proudly bears a unique weather vane in the shape of a model of the Fife yacht *Latifa* which once held the sailing record time for a transatlantic crossing.

From Fairlie Church, walk north along the pavement on the east side of the main road for 800 metres to the entrance road for Kelburn Country Park which leads up to Kelburn Castle, home of the Earl of Glasgow whose Boyle ancestors have held the estate since the 13th century. The double-headed eagle of their family crest was originally the emblem of a Norseman in Haco's fleet in 1263, which was assumed by the laird of Kelburn who slew him at the Battle of Largs. In 1703, David Boyle was created the first Earl of Glasgow in recognition of the major part he played in setting up the Act of Union, which ended the old Scots Parliament. The castle was built in 1581, and the old home farm now forms the centre of an attractive country park, with many activities for young and old, including a fine walk up the Kel Burn. In 2007, the castle walls made national news when a team of Brazilian artists were let loose to cover them entirely with murals.

Opposite the park entrance, walkers should follow the new cycle and walkers' path that leads under the railway to an established public footpath running between the railway and the marina boundary fence. This path is enhanced by a collection of 'Anchors, Floats, and Sinkers on loan to the Community from the Fairlie NATO Base', which are accompanied by explanatory notice boards. With some of the anchors weighing up to 8 tonnes, vandalism does not seem to be a problem; and it is unlikely that NATO will want them back now that the base is closed! There are two public car parks outwith the marina compound, giving pleasant access to both the shore and the attractive beach walk past The Pencil to the centre of Largs.

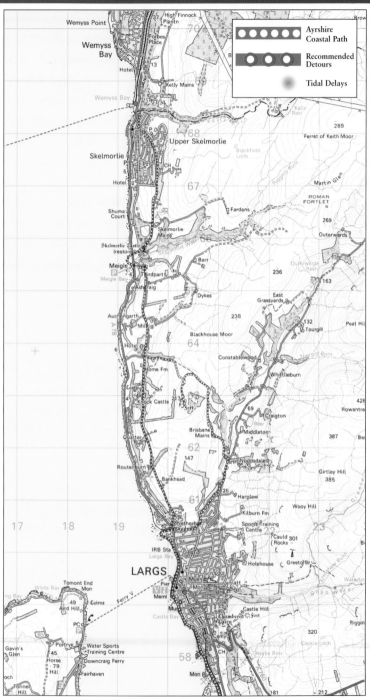

Ayrshire
Coastal Path

Recommended
Detours

Tidal Delays

12. The Pencil - LARGS Seafront - Largs Pier - Vikingar – then:-
a) 'High Road' up Noddsdale Water - Brisbane Glen Road - Brisbane Mains Farm - The Knock Hill – Blackhouse Burn – Red Road to SKELMORLIE - Kelly Burn and County Boundary

Distance = 15 km = 9.3 miles

6/5/11

Car Parks: **Largs Marina Public Car Park – Skelmorlie Station Road**

Walking Summary: *Moderate* - **pavements, paths, farm track, 200 m ascent, minor road, trunk road crossing**

b) 'Low Road' along Routenburn Road ((Red Road) - Knock Castle – Meigle – A78 (T) - Skelmorlie Bridge - Skelmorlie Castle - Red Road to SKELMORLIE - Kelly Burn and County Boundary

Distance = 11.5 km = 7.1 miles

Walking Summary: *Easy* – pavements, minor roads, trunk road crossing.

Points of Interest:

Transport:	Train service from Largs to Ayr and Glasgow Train service to Glasgow from Wemyss Bay Good bus service Ferry from Largs to Great Cumbrae Ferry from Wemyss Bay to Isle of Bute
Historical:	Site of Battle of Largs Neolithic chambered cairn Skelmorlie Aisle Vikingar Visitor Centre Netherhall - former home of Lord Kelvin Brisbane Glen - birthplace of Sir Thomas Makdougall Brisbane The Prophet's Grave The Knock - Iron Age vitrified fort
General:	Beach promenade Small visitor-friendly holiday resort Ferry to Cumbrae and round the island bicycle trip Trips on the *Waverley* RNLI Station Panoramic views from The Knock
Nature:	Coastal flora and fauna Marine Research Station on Cumbrae
Eating/Provisions:	Largs town centre shops, pubs and restaurants Skelmorlie shops and pubs
Public Toilets:	South Promenade Largs Pier Aubery Park Wemyss Bay Pier
Accommodation:	Largs B&Bs, hotels and guest houses Skelmorlie B&Bs, hotels and guest houses Skelmorlie Caravan and Campsite (Check www.ayrshirecoastalpath.org)

Largs (population 11241). Like so many other Ayrshire towns, Largs has an ancient and distinguished history - from Neolithic chambered cairns, Bronze Age sites, Iron Age forts, and Roman fortlets, through to the Battle of Largs and onwards to the holiday trippers of yesteryear. In medieval times, it was an isolated community, cut off from its hinterland by the massif of the Largs and Renfrewhire Hills, and from adjacent coastal neighbours in wintertime by floods on the Noddsdale and Gogo Burns. As a result, up until the eighteenth century, Largs traded more by sea with the Highlands across the Firth of Clyde than it did with the Lowlands overland.

Even so, Largs had no proper harbour or pier till an L-shaped pier was built in 1833, which was extended in 1847 as the Clyde steamer traffic expanded. At that time, Largs and Fairlie bays combined, held 34 herring boats, but during the popular Largs Fair in early June, these bays would be crowded with trading wherries and pleasure boats from Loch Fyne and Kintyre. With the advent of the steamer, Largs and Fairlie became very desirable places to live for rich Glasgow industrialists and merchants, who could now easily commute up-river to their businesses in the city.

The Pencil - Largs

An even more popular 'Doon the Watter' tradition became firmly established from the mid-19th century until the mid-20th century when, at weekends and during the Glasgow Fair holiday in late July, their workers also took advantage of the low prices engendered by fierce steamship company rivalry, to escape from city grime to the pleasures of the seaside. At its peak, in the 1890s, there were 42 passenger steamers plying the Firth of Clyde.

Today, only the *Waverley* remains. The world's last ocean-going paddle-steamer, she was built in 1947 to replace the old *Waverley* - which had been used as a minesweeper in the First World War, and which was sunk on active service at Dunkirk during WW2. Rescued from the breakers' yard twenty-five years ago and run by a dedicated band of steamer enthusiasts, the *Waverley* calls in regularly at Largs, Troon and Ayr during the summer season, and a trip on her is a must for any walkers wishing to experience the glorious bygone days of 'Sailin doon the Clyde'.

Following the opening of the Kilwinning-Ardrossan-Largs extension of the Ayr to Glasgow railway in 1885, Largs truly prospered as it opened its doors to holiday visitors; and resident merchants and professionals found their travelling time to Glasgow cut by several hours. By 1950 the population had reached 7400, and has since increased by another 50 per cent. Much of the local employment is still based on tourist or service industries, but, like other Ayrshire coastal towns, *'taking a house in Largs for the summer'* is a thing of the distant past.

Walking: From the Marina, it is only a short stroll to The Pencil, a striking memorial to Largs's greatest claim to fame - the Battle of Largs in October 1263, which ended for all time, Norway's claim to suzerainty over Scotland's western seaboard, largely dominated by the Vikings for almost 400 years.

At the age of twenty-three, King Alexander III of Scotland with a powerful force, had driven out from the Western Isles, the Norse Jarls who had refused to acknowledge him as their king. King Haco was furious and left Bergen with a huge fleet of galleys to re-establish control over the Hebrides. Having ravaged the west, he sailed round the Mull of Kintyre into the Clyde and attacked Ayr and many other coastal settlements - including an audacious sally down Loch Lomond after his warriors had dragged their long ships over the narrow isthmus between Arrochar and Tarbet.

With the Norse fleet anchored off the Cumbraes, Alexander cunningly played a waiting game and negotiated with the Norwegians till October arrived, when equinoctial gales drove some of Haco's ships across the Fairlie Roads, to ground in disarray upon the shore at Largs. The actual battle was not fought at The Pencil, but a few hundred metres north, where an ancient standing stone of conglomerate rock, situated on the grassy slope in front of Curling Hall flats, and inland of the only sandy beach at Largs suitable for beaching long ships, traditionally marks the site of the battle. *It apparently carried a plaque at one time but this has been stolen. This should be restored.* While the Norwegian Sagas describe an epic battle, the reality seems to have been more of a skirmish influenced by the weather. Whichever it may have been, the outcome was of huge significance for Scotland, freeing the west coast from Norse dominance and uniting the whole country for the first time under a strong ruler. King Haco died in Orkney on his journey back to Norway. The Viking warriors who died in battle, are said to have been buried on the Wee Cumbrae.

The original Curling Hall mansion was built for Dr John Cairnie, a one-armed, retired Indian Army doctor, sailor, and keen curler who in 1838 became the founder President of the Royal Caledonian Curling Club, now the world ruling body for the 'Roarin Game' - the sport of Curling. Cairnie is credited with building the world's first artificial outdoor ice rink in the grounds of Curling Hall, which later became a hotel and latterly was demolished to make way for modern flats.

Leaving behind the roar of battle on field or ice, the walker can enjoy tranquil views of the Big Cumbrae and a peaceful meander along the shore. Those of an inquiring mind and energetic enough to wish to visit 'Haco's Tomb' - in reality a Neolithic chambered cairn dating back 5000 years - should turn inland at a point where the vehicular road turns right and the promenade continues along to the jetty. Follow this road uphill then left for a few metres to reach May Street. Walk up May Street, over the railway bridge then through Anderson Park to the main road. Cross the road into Douglas Park and walk up the drive past the tennis courts following the signs to the chambered cairn - a round detour of about 1.3 km.

Return to the shore by the same route and stroll along the prom to pause for a moment on the Brisbane Bridge over the Gogo Burn, beyond which lie Largs pier and the attractive old town centre.

Largs from Aubrey Park

This bridge commemorates Sir Thomas Makdougall Brisbane, a distinguished general and keen amateur astronomer, who served under the Duke of Wellington before becoming the Governor of New South Wales in

1821. He was later in charge of the penal colony at Moreton Bay in Queensland from 1824-1939, and when that area became a free settlement in 1842, the town - now City of Brisbane - was named in his honour. His ancestral home, Brisbane Hall, lay 2 km up Brisbane Glen to the north of Largs. When it was demolished during the War, the main door was removed and shipped out to Queensland, where it is now part of Brisbane City Hall along with a portrait of Sir Thomas Makdougall Brisbane.

Bath Street provides a short cut through to Main Street and the town centre. On the right is a magnificent red sandstone church with a tall and elegant spire - the Clark Memorial Church - built in 1890 and gifted by John Clark, the Paisley owner of Anchor Threads. In the old Largs churchyard just off Main Street behind The George, situated among the venerable tombstones is the weathered headstone of Dr John Cairnie of Curling Hall. Beyond it is the Skelmorlie Aisle, the mausoleum of the Montgomeries of Skelmorlie Castle, with its fine painted ceiling (1636) and canopied tomb which is now cared for by Historic Scotland and open to the public; and also the smaller Brisbane Aisle with memorial plaques to Sir Thomas and his family.

The centre of old Largs is an atmospheric clutter of early 19th century buildings with narrow winds and back closes, and lots of eating places scattered among the shops. Round the corner at the Pierhead in marked contrast stands The Moorings, a striking new development, built in 1990, with its sharp ship's prow corner thrusting towards the open sea.

The ferry across to Cumbrae leaves every half hour, and gives walkers an opportunity to visit this delightful small island, hire a bicycle in Millport, and spend a few hours cycling round its 16 km coastline, while absorbing the diversity of its abundant flora and fauna. The Marine Research Institute and Aquarium is well worth a 'stop and see'.

Largs ferries

In summer the area round Largs pier is always busy with the usual seaside amusements and boating trips, but this frenetic activity quickly dissipates, giving way to the more peaceful pursuits of 'just daunerin', or sitting watching the world go by, as the broad promenade curves gently round Largs Bay.

Halfway along Largs Bay is the RNLI Inshore Lifeboat Slip. This has an interesting history as it was originally built during the Second World War to bring ashore Catalina flying boats for repair and maintenance. These seaplanes were used by Coastal Command to spot and attack German U-boats lurking in the North Channel Approaches to the Firth of Clyde. For any submarines that did manage to penetrate the Clyde, a series of anti-submarine wire-cable booms were stretched across the main channel north of Largs to protect huge convoys assembling at the Tail o the Bank, just off Greenock. The old site where the Catalinas were serviced on the opposite side of the A78, is now occupied by *Vikingar* the new Viking Heritage Centre - a salient reminder of a much earlier conflict and one of Largs's main tourist attractions, which is well worth the admission fee.

Returning to the shore path, follow it along to Aubery Park. On summer Sunday and Wednesday afternoons, members of Largs Model Boat Club sail their superb model craft on the boating pond to the delight of passers-by, old and young. After crossing the main A78 (T) a short distance inland from the mouth of the Noddsdale Water, walkers now have the choice of a **High Road** or a **Low Road**, for the final section of the Ayrshire coastal path to Skelmorlie.

a) The High Road - for more energetic walkers – turns right and passes through Barr Crescent, from where it follows a path alongside the south bank of the burn. High on the hill slope on the north side is Netherhall, once the home of Professor Sir William Thomson of Glasgow University, later Lord Kelvin of Largs - the world-renowned scientist and mathematician. A pioneer in the new science of thermo-dynamics, he postulated in 1848 the theory of 'absolute zero' temperature; and the SI unit of temperature - the 'kelvin' - is named after him. His experimental work on the electrical properties of cables led to the laying of the first transatlantic telegraph cable in 1866 - and a knighthood.

After 1.5 km, the burnside path joins the Brisbane Glen Road just short of Brisbane Bridge. Beside the bridge is a cairn and plaque presented by the City of Brisbane in 1989 to commemorate Sir Thomas Makdougall Brisbane. Although his birthplace - Brisbane Hall - is long since demolished, a farm road about 300 metres further on leads off to Brisbane Mains Farm on the lower slopes of The Knock. A signpost here denotes the Knock Hill section of the Ayrshire Coastal Path, and marker posts are placed at regular intervals along this track to the top. A short distance further up the Noddsdale road - the original old high road from Largs to Greenock - is the Prophet's Grave. Buried here is the Rev William Smith who refused to leave his parishioners during a plague epidemic in 1647, and tended the sick and dying till he himself caught the disease and died. Two holly trees were planted, on either side of his grave, and it was prophesied that the plague would never return to Largs as long as their branches were not allowed to meet.

Brisbane Mains, with its clock tower and arched entrance into a square courtyard, is typical of many mains farms built on Scottish 18th century estates. *It is still a working farm, and walkers are advised not to take dogs on this section of the Path over Knock Hill because of the risk to sheep and lambs in the spring – and in the summer months, a real risk to walkers with dogs from angry cows seeking to protect their young calves on the hill pastures.*

Passing through the kissing gate by the farm, follow the track that traverses north and then northwest up the hillside. In rainy weather, this track, though metalled with gravel, is wet and muddy in places. After about 1.4 km, a spur turns west then south and does a clockwise spiral to the summit. Apparently in the 19th century, the ladies from Brisbane House would be driven up here by carriage for a picnic while their men were shooting game in the estate below. The final easy ascent of this grassy path as it winds up and round to the triangulation point (217 m) past an interesting outcrop of lava rocks, provides an ever-revealing and fascinating view of the Firth of Clyde. The name Knock is simply the Gaelic *cnoc* = hill. On the summit is an impressive Iron Age vitrified hill fort, whose ramparts and outer walls would have been crowned by wooden pallisades. Built for defence in time of inter-tribal wars, the local population would have fled their homes in the glen to seek shelter within its walls on the approach of an enemy force.

Skelmorlie and Cowal Hills from Knock Hill

The panorama from the top is stupendous - which is simply the reason why our reluctant walker has been dragged up here in the first place. Not only is there a great retrospective view to the south, of Largs and much of the terrain already tramped; but there are magnificent prospects to the west over the sail-dotted Firth of Clyde to Bute and the Cowal Hills, and northwards over Skelmorlie and the 600 foot chimney of Inverkip power station, past the western rim of the Greenock hills to the Upper Firth, the Holy Loch and Loch Long. Stretching far to the east rise the sheep hills and grouse moors of the Clyde Muirshiel Regional Park.

Coming off the summit, follow the track back down to a marker post at the point nearest the march dyke to the west and follow this dyke north for 200 m to a kissing gate beside an iron gate. From here a pleasant Path descends along the edge of a beech shelter-belt bordering the Blackhouse Burn to join the 'Red Road', a local name for the old coastal high road which runs north to Skelmorlie and onwards to Gourock and Greenock. The name seems strange now, till a glance at the roadside ditches provide a clue. They are filled with old red sandstone silt from the surrounding fields, which must have tinted the rough surface of the road before it was macadamised. To the south, half-hidden in the woods, is the 19th century Knock Castle, which replaced an earlier 400 year old tower house. To the north is Manor Park, now a hotel, which dates from 1843.

Blackhouse Glen

b) The Low Road – for gentle walkers – turns left on crossing the A78 (T) and follows Routenburn Road in a gradual ascent along the Red Road which traverses the hillside for 3 km - giving superb views of the Firth below – till it is rejoined by the High Road near a minor road junction at Blackhouse Burn. Both continue northwards along the road for another 2 km till it drops down into the hamlet of Meigle at the foot of Skelmorlie Water. Although this is normally a very quiet road, walkers are advised to keep a lookout for horses as well as cars. *If the main A78 coast road is blocked by a road accident or gale-borne waves, the Red Road can become busy and potentially dangerous with diverted traffic.*

At Meigle, unfortunately, the dangers of the busy A78 (T) have now to be faced since there is no pavement on the east side to take the walker safely along to the Skelmorlie Castle Road 150 metres to the north. It is necessary therefore to cross smartly and alertly over to the seaward side of the main road, from where, walkers - with their backs to the traffic - could use a narrow pavement, which for some obscure reason stops a full 30m short of the Skelmorlie Castle road end.

A more pleasant alternative would be to follow the rough path leading down from the north end of the bridge on to the foreshore. On a good day this might just be a pleasant spot to have a lunch break and enjoy the fine views across to Bute and Cowal , before walking round the grass and shingle banks to emerge right opposite the next road end.

Re-cross the A78(T) safely and climb this minor road that rises steeply past Skelmorlie Castle and then travels for a kilometre through open countryside, passing Skelmorlie Caravan and Campsite before it reaches the outskirts of Upper Skelmorlie. Skelmorlie Castle, an ancestral home of the Montgomeries, was built around 1502, and like so many other tower houses, was altered and extended several times. Following a fire in 1959, a large Victorian wing was demolished and the building has regained the more pleasing lines of its 16th century tower house.

Skelmorlie (Population 1828) only dates from the 1840s when land was feued to build houses for wealthy city merchants who would be able to catch the early Glasgow steamer from Wemyss Bay. The original Victorian villas were crammed on a narrow raised beach beneath rugged old sandstone cliffs peppered with sea caves. Very quickly however, the village outgrew itself and more fine mansions were built on the cliff tops, with wonderful views across to the Cowal peninsula. Upper Skelmorlie has continued to expand and maintain its reputation as a fine place to live.

Passing the strenuous-looking golf course up on the hillside to the right, the Path route gradually descends through the upper village. Opposite a sign for the bowling green, Station Road winds down to reach the bridge over the Kelly Burn, beyond which is the pier and station at Wemyss Bay - and the opportunity to take a ferry to Rothesay and walk round the beautiful island of Bute. Kelly Burn marks the Ayrshire-Renfrewshire boundary, and sadly and abruptly, the end of the Ayrshire Rotary Coastal Path.

We hope that walkers have enjoyed this walk through time; living through their imagination, some of the turbulent and powerful history of the Cradle of Scots Independence; savouring the beauty of every mile of this wonderful historic coastline with hidden surprises round every headland; observing the diversity and abundance of its flora and fauna; and learning much about those Ayrshire folk over the centuries, who have done so much to influence both the course of Scottish and world history, and many aspects of our modern way of life.

ACKNOWLEDGEMENTS

First and foremost, we cannot thank enough all those farmers and landowners without whose gracious and pragmatic acceptance of walkers crossing their land, the formation of this long-distance Ayrshire Coastal Path could not have taken place. Thanks also to Turnberry, St Nicholas, Prestwick and Royal Troon Golf Clubs for their cooperation and positive help in routing the Path through their courses; and to the National Trust for Scotland for the route through Culzean.

Crucial to this process was the support of Past-President John Davidson, whose wide experience as a Senior Agricultural Officer in Ayrshire brought an invaluable element of professionalism and trust into our discussions - and gate contract agreements - with many of his former clients.

From the very earliest stages of the project till its conclusion, the professional advice and wholehearted support of David Gray, Countryside Access Officer for South Ayrshire Council, was invaluable. His memorable words - 'Let's go for it!' prompted our decision to do just that.

The quiet professionalism of Louise Kirk, his counterpart on North Ayrshire Council, proved equally helpful in establishing contacts in her area, promoting the Path within North Ayrshire Council, and sourcing support and grant funding.

We must especially thank ENTRUST, which oversees the allocation of Landfill Tax revenue to environmental projects; and the major support of the Trustees of South Ayrshire Waste Environmental Trust (SAWET) and of Fiona Ross, their Administrator, who allocated £40,000 of Landfill Tax money for the main Coastal Path construction work in South Ayrshire; and also North Ayrshire Council's Landfill Tax Fund, which granted £6,000 through ENTRUST for work in the North.

South Ayrshire Rural Communities Committee were very supportive in allocating £6000, and likewise the North Ayrshire Community Outdoor Access Grant Scheme who contributed £500 towards our Website.

Our thanks to Scottish Natural Heritage and their Area Manager, John Collie, for his helpful advice and considerable support throughout - and his assistance in securing £14,000 from SNH for path work and signage county-wide.

As well as sterling support for muddy path clearance and construction work from a loyal corps of physically active members of Ayr Rotary Club, there were other members active in securing funding for publication of the Guide Book. The ARCPG thanks all those Rotarians who helped for their support.

In addition to John Davidson, the ARCPG comprised Rtn Willie Watters whose experience as a walk leader was useful in mapping, setting up our publicity Power Point Presentation, and assisting with compilation of signage from Glenapp to Skelmorlie; Past-President Neil Beattie coordinated details with his daughter Jennifer Beattie who designed and produced our superb Website; Past-President Alistair Tyre used his administrative expertise to organise the publicity and details for the official Ayrshire Coastal Path launch in June 2008; Past-President Alec Thomson balanced the books to the last penny; and finally, special mention must be made of Archie McGregor, who as a retired civil engineer but no longer a Rotarian, dedicated many professional and physical hours to overseeing the engineering works so crucial to the success of the Path.

Our thanks are also due to members of the Rotary Clubs of Girvan, Alloway, Prestwick and Troon - and all their organised volunteers from the local communities - who assisted in the first Great Rotary Beach Clean, and who are keen to do it again . . . and again!

Our Contractors and Suppliers deserve special mention:

> The volunteer teams of British Trust for Conservation Volunteers and Scottish Wildlife Trust who assisted with path construction and strimming.

> Chris Reid, Maybole –'Digger Dan' – helpful and obliging, and a fine digger operator.

> Jim McCreadie, Maybole and Campbell Crawford, Largs – skilled fencers –'aye lookin for the answers an no the problems'.

> Simon Phillips of Sustrans, for many cooperative hours preparing joint signage on the NCN7 and 73 cycle routes; and Blair Wyllie of South Ayrshire Roads Dept for designing all the road signs.

> Metrosigns of Bradford: Border Signs and Graphics, Dumfries; Dee-organ, Paisley - for prompt and helpful service in providing our waymarker discs, marker posts, and signage; and Barr Quarries, Solway Precast, and Jewson's – for discounts and donations of materials.

And finally, our gratitude to Graeme Ferguson and Kenny Dickson of Kestrel Press for turning a plain manuscript and amateur collection of photographs into a highly professional and most attractive Guide Book.

BIBLIOGRAPHY

While the compilation of much of this guide is the result of first hand observation, glaring gaps in the author's knowledge of certain locales and the rigorous cross-checking of supposed facts, required a considerable amount of delving into numerous books and monographs about Ayrshire. The author would like to acknowledge the help he received from the following sources:

Ayrshire - Its History and Historic Families by William Robertson (1908)

Ayrshire - The Third Statistical Account by John Strawhorn (1950)

Discovering Ayrshire by John Strawhorn and Ken Andrew (1994)

Ayrshire Heritage by Andrew Boyle (1990)

Ayrshire and Arran - An Illustrated Architectural Guide by Rob Close (1992)

The Royal Burgh of Ayr by Annie I Dunlop (1953)

Ayrshire Coast by Dane Love (2001)

Old Fairlie by Frank Donnachie

This Time of Crisis - The West of Scotland in WW2 by Andrew Jeffrey (1993)

The Scottish Census 2001

Walking and Cycling Pamphlets by South and North Ayrshire Councils

Birds of Ayrshire – A County Checklist – by Angus Hogg (1983)

Nature Reserve Pamphlets by the Scottish Wildlife Trust

The following monographs of the Ayrshire Archaeological and Natural History Society :

A New Map of Ayrshire by Captain Armstrong and Son (1775)

The Bronze Age in Ayrshire by Alex Morrison (1978)

Old Ayrshire Harbours by Angus Graham (1984)

Smuggling and the Ayrshire Economic Boom by L M Cullen (1994)

The Port of Ayr 1727 - 1780 by Eric J Graham (1995)

John Smith of Dalry, Geologist, Antiquarian and Natural Historian (1995)

Robert Reid Cunninghame of Seabank House by Eric J Graham (1997)

Historic Ayr, Historic Alloway, Historic Prestwick - Guides for Visitors (1998-2003)

APPENDIX I TIDAL INFORMATION

High Tides occur twice a day, approximately 12 hours apart. It then takes about 6 hours for the sea to drop to Low Tide level, and 6 hours to rise again to the next High Tide.

High Tide Level (from 2.1-3.5m / 8.2-12.8ft) is *the height of the tide above a baseline called Chart Datum* (the lowest ever recorded low tide for the area). So the height of a high tide can vary by as much as 1.4m /4.6ft during the course of the year.

The biggest High Tides - called 'Spring Tides' - occur twice each month for about a week at the time of the New Moon and Full Moon on a 29-day Lunar Calendar cycle. The highest Spring Tides (3.3 - 3.4m = orange and red blocks) occur fortunately in late Autumn and Winter (November – February), when fewer walkers are likely to be out and about.

The lowest Spring Tides are in the early Summer months (May to July), when most High Tide Levels are around or below 2.7m (white). This is the level below which most of the marked 'Tidal Passage Delay' areas can be walked without problems.

Fig 1. Typical Example of the Pattern of Daytime Spring Tides over a full year.

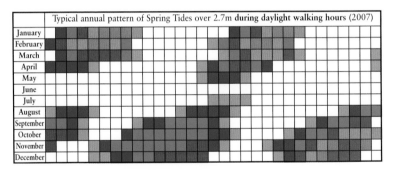

The lowest High Tides - called 'Neap Tides' - also occur twice monthly for about a week at the time of the half moon. Most of the time, High Tide Levels at Neaps are below 2.7m (white) and there are no Tidal Passage Delays.

Fig.2 Passage Delay Tide Heights to be used in conjunction with
Admiralty Easy Tide Tables **FOR AYR.**

Passage Delay Tide Heights.	Water Depth above boot soles.		Rising Tide Delay Time taken for tide to rise above 2.7m passable level to High Tide and back	Falling Tide Delay Time taken for tide to drop from HW to passable 2.7m level.
3.4m	0.7m (crotch)		4hr 20m	2hr 10m
3.3m	0.6m (thigh)		4hr 00m	2hr 00m
3.2m	0.5m (crotch)		3hr 40m	1hr 50m
3.1m	0.4m (knee)		3hr 20m	1hr 40m
3.0m	0.3m (calf)		3hr 00m	1hr 30m
2.9m	0.2m		2hr 20m	1hr 10m
2.8m	0.1m (ankle)		1hr 40m	0hr 50m
2.7m	0m (sole)		0hr	0hr
0.4-1.4m	Low Tide			

Useful Tide Marker -

Rung 6 = 3.3 m (Ayr)

Rung 10 = 2.8 m (Ayr)

Dunure Harbour - ladder in SW corner:

At High Water, Drumbain and Isle Port are impassable for next 2 hours (takes 45min - 1hr to get there)

On a falling tide, Drumbain and Isle Port are now passable for many hours
On a rising tide, both sites will be impassable in the 45min to 1hr time taken to get there.

Height (m)

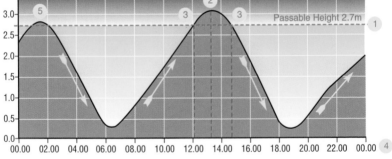

Passable Height 2.7m

Friday 14 March

HW	LW	HW	LW
01:19	06:48	13:22	18:59
2.8m	0.3m	3.1m	0.2m

1. Draw line on graph at 2.7m.
2. High Tide is at 13.22hrs.
3. Impassable between 12.15-14.45hrs.
4. Add 1hr during British Summertime (eg 13.22 + 1hr = 14.22hrs.
5. Previous High Tide was almost passable.

GENERAL GUIDANCE NOTES FOR TIDAL PASSAGE DELAY POINTS:

If planning a walk that will involve negotiating one of the marked 'Tidal Passage Delay' sections on the route, it is essential to do the following:

1. **Compare your walk times and ETA with the** time **and** level **of High Tide for the day of your outing on the Admiralty Easytide website (www.easytide.ukho.gov.uk) or alternatively BBC Weather (www.bbc.co.uk/tides).**
   N.B. Times and Depths **are approximate. Deep low pressure and strong winds can raise tide levels by 0.2 - 0.3 m.**

2. State of the Tide: **Any tide height** below a level of 2.6-2.7m **means an unrestricted passage along most of the Ayrshire Coast. If possible, try to plan your walk on a falling tide e.g. -**

   Walking window on a falling tide - Time from 2.7 m to LW and back to 2.7 m = 9 h 30 m

   Walking window on a rising tide - Time from LW to 2.7 m and impassable = 4 h 45 m

SPECIFIC TIDAL PASSAGE DELAY POINTS:

Greenan Castle, Ayr - a tide level of 3.0 m (Ayr) or below is passable. *Alternative route*: Path up to Greenan Castle and follow NCN7 track to Doonfoot

Heads of Ayr (East) - a tide level of 3.0 m (Ayr) or below is passable. *Alternative route*: Nil. May have to wade or wait at West end for 1-3 hrs going south.

Heads of Ayr (West) - a tide level of 2.8 m (Ayr) or below is passable. *Alternative route*: Nil. Will have to wade or wait

Drumbain - a tide level of 2.8 m (Ayr) or below is passible. *Alternative route*: Nil. A private path up the glen leads into Drumbain garden, and the north side of the glen also leads into a private cottage garden. Wade or wait.

Isle Port at Croy - a tide level of 2.7 m (Ayr) or below is passable. *Alternative route*: Nil. The Caravan Site is private property with no through access. Wade or wait.

Milton Burn, Turnberry - a tide level of 2.6 m (Ayr) or below is passable. *Alternative route*: Wait, or follow the burn up to the first bridge.

Dipple Burn, ISP Aginates - a tide level of 2.7 m (Ayr) or below is passable. *Alternative route*: Wait or wade. The A77T roadside is dangerous and not advised.

Curragh Cottages - a tide level of 2.0 m (Ayr) or below is passable. *Alternative route*: Field edge path through k/gates for 500 m behind Curragh Cottages.

Variable tide levels on short stretches of beach between Lendalfoot and Girvan. *Alternative route*: Roadside pavement or verge beside the A77T.

APPENDIX II - CHECKLIST OF CLYDE COASTAL PATH BIRDS

Because of its compact size, and the amazing diversity of terrain and habitat experienced when travelling even short distances, Scotland plays host to a far greater number of bird species than would be found if travelling over the same distance in the USA, Australia, or continental Europe.

The diversity of terrain encountered while traversing the Clyde Coastal Path mirrors that of Scotland itself, and the sea and seashore, the cliffs, the hills and moors, the rivers and estuaries, woodlands and open pastures all have their favoured bird species. Many species can be found in several habitats at different times of the year. For example, many upland birds migrate to feed on the coast during the winter months - along with migrants from northern Europe and Iceland - and in summer, birds which nest in trees or bushes may also be seen foraging for food in open fields and pasture.

On a good spring day it should be possible to record 40 - 50 bird species during the course of a day's walk. To help the casual birdwatcher/walker and stranger to the area, this checklist has been sub-divided into the various habitats in which the various species are most likely to be seen. The seasons in which they may be found is also given, as well as whether they are common or rare.

135 species have been listed, but many others - only very rarely recorded - have not. Let them come as a surprise to observant birdwatchers.

*	Common	R	Resident species	S	Summer Visitor
**	Less Common	W	Winter Visitor	P	Passage migrants
***	Rare				

Offshore birds:

***	Red-throated River	W	Dipple. Turnberry. Doonfoot
***	Black-throated Diver	P	Spring passage Dipple to Stevenston
***	Great Northern Diver	W	Dipple Shore. Turnberry Point
**	Little Grebe	W	River estuaries. Troon Harbour
**	Great Crested Grebe	W	Barassie Shore to Ardeer
***	Red-necked Grebe	W	Barassie Shore
***	Slavonian Grebe	W	Portencross
*	Manx Shearwater	S	Well offshore. Irvine Bay Turnberry
**	Storm Petrel	S	Inshore after westerly gales
*	Gannet	S	All along the coast
**	Scaup	W	Ayr Bay and Barassie
***	Long-tailed Duck	W	Turnberry to Irvine Bay
**	Common Scoter	W	Maidens. Ayr and Irvine Bays
*	Guillemot	S	All along the coast
*	Razorbill	S	All along the coast
**	Kittiwake	S	Well offshore

CLYDE COASTAL PATH BIRDS

Inshore birds:

*	Grey Heron	R	River estuaries and wetlands
*	Mute Swan	R	Culzean. River mouths
**	Greylag Goose	W	Near Hunterston
**	Shelduck	R	Dipple to north of Ardrossan
**	Wigeon	W	River estuaries and wetlands
*	Teal	W	River estuaries and wetlands
*	Mallard	R	River estuaries and wetlands
**	Pintail	W	Culzean. Doonfoot. Barassie
**	Shoveler	W	Culzean
**	Tufted Duck	W	Culzean. Ayr Bay. Shewalton Ponds
*	Eider	R	All along the coast.
**	Goldeneye	W	Dipple to Barassie. Doonfoot
*	Red-breasted Merganser	R	All along the coast.
**	Arctic Skua	S	Barassie. Horse Island
**	Great Skua	S	Barassie.
*	Black-headed Gull	R	All along the coast
*	Common Gull	R	All along the coast
*	Lesser Black-backed Gull	R	All along the coast
*	Herring Gull	R	All along the coast
***	Iceland Gull	W	Fishing Harbours
***	Glaucous Gull	W	Fishing Harbours
*	Great Black-backed Gull	R	All along the coast
**	Sandwich Tern	S	Lady Isle and Horse Island
*	Common Tern	S	All along the coast
**	Arctic Tern	S	Lady Isle and Horse Island
**	Little Tern	S	Ballantrae
**	Black Guillemot	R	Troon harbour

Cliff birds:

**	Buzzard	R	Above escarpments and cliffs
*	Kestrel	R	All along the coast
**	Peregrine	R	Above sea cliffs
**	Fulmar	S	Cliffs near Ballantrae. Culzean
*	Cormorant	R	Cliffs south of Ballantrae
*	Shag	R	Cliffs south of Ballantrae
*	Rock Dove	R	All cliff areas
**	Raven	R	South Ayrshire cliffs. Culzean

Hill/Moor Birds:

**	Red Grouse	R	Glenapp moors
*	Curlew	R	Estuaries and moorland
**	Short-eared Owl	R	Glenapp and Largs moors
*	Meadow Pipit	R	All upland areas
*	Wheatear	R	Glenapp and Largs moors

Shoreline and Estuary Birds:

**	Merlin	W	Scarce coastal visitor
*	Oystercatcher	R	All along the coast
*	Ringed Plover	R	Shingle beaches and estuaries
*	Golden Plover	W	Dipple. Doonfoot. Barassie
**	Grey Plover	W	Dipple and Barassie shores
*	Lapwing	W	All along the coast. Pastureland
**	Knot	W	Prestwick to Stevenston
**	Sanderling	P	Sandy beaches, spring /autumn
**	Purple Sandpiper	W	Rocky shores along coast
*	Dunlin	W	All along the coast
*	Snipe	W	Wetland areas
**	Black-tailed Godwit	P	Autumn - Barassie, Hunterston
**	Bar-tailed Godwit	W	Dipple, Prestwick, Barassie
**	Whimbrel	P	Along coast, spring and autumn
**	Spotted Redshank	P	Autumn Doonfoot. Shewalton. Irvine
*	Redshank	W	Shores and estuaries
**	Greenshank	W	Muddy shores and estuaries
*	Common Sandpiper	P	Autumn. Coast. Breeds on rivers
*	Turnstone	W	Rocky and shingle beaches
*	Rock Pipit	R	Rocky coastline
*	Pied Wagtail	R	All along the coast
**	Stonechat	R	Scattered along the coast
*	Whinchat	R	Scattered along the coast
*	Jackdaw	R	Estuaries and seaweed wrack
*	Carrion Crow	R	All along the coast

River Birds:

**	Swift	S	Town areas of River Ayr
**	Kingfisher	R	River Doon
*	Sand Martin	S	Rivers and ponds
*	Swallow	S	Rivers and ponds
*	House Martin	S	Rivers and ponds
*	Grey Wagtail	R	River Doon
*	Dipper	R	River Doon

Scrub and Woodland Birds:

*	Sparrowhawk	R	Woodland and scrub
*	Pheasant	R	Wood margins and stubble fields
**	Stock Dove	R	Hunterston
*	Wood Pigeon	R	All along the coast
*	Collared Dove	R	Mainly suburban areas
**	Barn Owl	R	Uncommon
**	Tawny Owl	R	Woodland sites
*	Wren	R	All woodland and scrub areas
*	Dunnock	R	Wooded and suburban areas
*	Robin	R	Woodland and scrub

*	Blackbird	R	Wooded and open coastal areas
*	Song Thrush	R	Wooded and open coastal areas
* *	Mistle Thrush	R	Woodlands
* *	Whitethroat	S	Coastal scrubland
* *	Garden Warbler	S	Stinchar and Girvan valleys
* *	Blackcap	S	More common south of Ayr
*	Chiffchaff	S	Culzean woodlands
*	Willow Warbler	S	All areas
* *	Goldcrest	R	Coniferous woodland
* *	Spotted Flycatcher	S	Open woodland
* *	Long-tailed Tit	R	Wooded areas
*	Coal Tit	R	Coniferous woods and suburbs
*	Blue Tit	R	Deciduous woodland and suburbs
*	Great Tit	R	Wooded areas and suburbs
* *	Treecreeper	R	Wooded areas
* *	Jay	R	River Doon
*	Magpie	R	Common from Ayr northwards
*	Chaffinch	R	Woodland and hedgerows
*	Greenfinch	R	Woodlands and hedgerows
*	Goldfinch	R	Coastal scrubland and pasture
* *	Siskin	R	Coniferous woods and suburbs
*	Linnet	R	Coastal scrubland and pasture
* *	Bullfinch	R	River valleys and conifers
*	Redpoll	R	Coastal scrubland and pasture
* *	Yellowhammer	R	Hedgerows and scrubland

Wetlands Birds:

*	Moorhen	R	Culzean. Rivers and ponds
*	Coot	R	Culzean. Shewalton ponds
*	Sedge Warbler	R	Wetlands and pond margins
* *	Reed Bunting	R	Wetlands and pond margins

Open Pasture Birds:

* *	Partridge	R	Girvan valley
*	Cuckoo	S	All along the coast
*	Skylark	R	All along the coast
*	Fieldfare	W	Open fields and hedgerows
*	Redwing	W	Open fields and hedgerows
*	Rook	R	Arable fields and wrack
*	Starling	R	Open fields and towns
*	House Sparrow	R	Farmyards, stubble, and towns

Other Recorded species: . . . .

. . . .

. . . .

. . . .

APPENDIX III

1. STRANRAER TO GLENAPP LINK PATH

The Rotary Cub of Stranraer is actively surveying and developing a 10 mile coastal path to link The Southern Upland Way and the town of Stranraer with the Ayrshire Coastal Path at Glenapp

The route has been agreed with all the landowners involved, and preliminary work on sourcing grants and contractors is being undertaken at time of publication.

From Stranraer it runs along the eastern shore of Loch Ryan, using a combination of old railway track, existing roadside paths and shoreline until it passes Cairnryan. Just north of Cairnryan it will cross the A77(T) and traverse up past Lairds Hill to follow the forest edge round the hillside above Glenapp, before dropping down to Glenapp Kirk and the start of the Coastal Path.

When completed, this fine route promises to provide walkers with magnificent views across Loch Ryan to the Rhinns of Galloway, and beyond to the County Down coastline of Northern Ireland, as well as touching on some of Galloway's rich archeological and more recent history.

2. WEMYSS BAY - CLYDE MUIRSHIEL PARK - ERSKINE BRIDGE - FORTH AND CLYDE CANAL - GLASGOW

The Rotary Club of Gourock is in the preliminary stage of deciding to develop this route which will effectively provide a link between the Ayrshire Coastal Path, the Upper Clyde Glasgow, and the West Highland Way. Watch this space!

1. *Rotarians and rubbish from Heads of Ayr*
2. *Beach clean at Bracken Bay*
3. *Willie Watters and Craig Tara staff*

4. *Scottish Wildlife Team*
5. *Clearing the jungle*
6. *Same area cleared*
7. *Dumping 80 tonnes of ballast*
8. *The end in sight*

9. *First sods cut at foot of gully*
10. *Ankle deep in glaur at top of gully*
11. *Step laying a few weeks later*
12. *Men at work - Colin Mearns - The Herald*

BEACH CLEAN

BRACKEN BAY PATH

FISHERTON GULLY PATH